## Praise for Take-Charge Living

[*Take-Charge Living*] is a remarkable book that provides a clearly presented set of effective strategies to guide one's journey into fulfillment and meaningful relationships with others. The reader will develop the self-confidence to take charge of his or her life and achieve a sense of empowerment and sequential mastery during the life cycle.

*-Joseph L. White, Ph.D.*
*Professor Emeritus of Psychology and Psychiatry at the University of California, Irvine.*
*author of Promising Practices in Multicultural Competency Training*

... offers a practical, rational and honest way to reach our most cherished dreams and goals. You are in expert hands, as Dr. Jacobs dispels the illusion that "some of us have what it takes to change, and some of us don't." She shines the light of understanding on the actual and repeatable steps that lead to successful living. You will be amazed at the strength that will arise and the inspiration that will come as a result of you taking charge.

*-Susan McNeal Velasquez – President of Unleash The Power of Your Intuition Seminars and author of Beyond Intellect: Journey Into the Wisdom of Your Intuitive Mind*

Provides practical, easy-to-follow steps to help us attain the goals we have struggled to reach. Its particular strength is in fully exploring barriers and resistance to change. Dr. Jacobs provides guidelines for understanding and overcoming those common impediments that so often stop us from fully realizing our goals and dreams.

*-Jill Waterman, Ph.D., Adjunct Professor of Psychology at UCLA*
*Coordinator, UCLA Psychology Clinic*
*Author of Helping At-Risk Students: A Group Counseling Approach for Grades 6-9.*

Presents clear, concise, practical steps for gaining insight into one's own behavior and greater control over one's life.  Dr. Jacobs takes an optimistic view of human nature that leaves the reader with enhanced thinking skills and increased self-confidence.

*-Lee Winocur Field, Ph.D., former President and Executive Director of the Center for the Teaching of Thinking and author of Impact Thinking and Laboratory Activities to Understand and Nurture Choices.*

The book and podcast series, like Marion herself, is credible, important and friendly. It speaks to the part of us that is still waiting for permission to live our life our way and to get beyond the need for proof via our feelings that we can evolve into who we want to be. I spent many hours with Marion Jacobs in the production of the podcasts based on the book, and from this I know that she lives of what she speaks.

*-Allan Hunkin, President of SuccessTalk Channels*

Dr. Marion Jacobs has succeeded brilliantly in translating the process of self-empowerment into an inspiring yet practical, guide for anyone seeking positive behavior change.  Dr. Jacobs encourages the reader to maintain a "stay in support of myself" stance while guiding us to awareness and understanding of our unique thoughts and beliefs that keep us stuck in frustrating and self-defeating cycles of behavior.  *Take Charge Living* is the therapist you've been looking for to help you actually succeed in growing a little more each day into the person you want to be.

*-Rita Milhollin, Ph.D., Counseling Psychologist and Lecturer in Social Ecology (Ret.), University of California, Irvine*

Dr. Jacobs is the consummate professional. Her diligence in research is equaled by her compassion and acumen as a clinician. She is a compelling author and a dedicated, natural teacher with the ability to turn students on to the even the most arcane.

*-O. Lee Trick, MD., Psychiatrist and Co-Director Family Institute of the Southwest*

Marion Jacobs provides intimacy via the written word. To "everyperson" Dr Jacobs presents hope of change.Today people are craving global and American hope for positive change and that includes at its base hope for personal change

*-Reita A.Troum, LCSW, Educator and Psychotherapist, Co-Director Family Institute of The Southwest*

Jacobs shows her readers how to overcome their own resistance to changing unwanted behavior--or beliefs -even emotions ... Best of all, the book can be used in little digestible pieces.

*-Gerald Goodman, Professor Emeritus, Psychology, UCLA*

A straightforward, practical toolkit for identifying and overcoming barriers to change...What distinguishes this book from much self-help hokum is the realistic discussion of the intense negative feelings that often arise from enacting change, and the techniques required for withstanding those feelings and moving forward. ...A self-help book that could actually work.

*—Kirkus Discoveries*

# Take Charge Living

# Take Charge Living

## How to Recast Your Role in Life...
## One Scene At A Time

*Marion Kramer Jacobs, Ph.D.*

With a Foreword by Dr. Manuel J. Smith,
best-selling author of When I Say No I Feel Guilty

iUniverse, Inc.
New York Bloomington

**Take-Charge Living:**
**How to Recast Your Role in Life...One Scene At A Time**



*iUniverse books may be ordered through booksellers or by contacting:*

*iUniverse*
*1663 Liberty Drive, Suite 200*
*Bloomington, IN 47403*
*www.iuniverse.com*
*1-800-Authors (1-800-288-4677)*

*ISBN: 978-1-60528-014-1 (pbk)*
*ISBN: 978-0-595-61296-3 (ebk)*

*Printed in the United States of America*

*This book is dedicated with love and affection to my parents, Edith and Milton Kramer, my sister, Leslie Kramer, and my life partner, James B. Willis Jr. for their love, inspiration, support, and wisdom.*

The moment of change is the only poem.

Adrienne Rich

# *Contents*

# *Acknowledgments*

It's a long road from thinking about writing a book to seeing it in print. How fortunate I was to have help and encouragement all along the way from some very wonderful and talented people. With appreciation I particularly acknowledge:

James Belmont Willis Jr., Leslie Kramer, Diane Mason, Alesandra Lanto, Rita Milhollin, Adel Martinez, Suzanne Esko, Gerald Goodman and Mayra Gutierrez, for their ongoing love, encouragement and valuable feedback.

Patricia Snell, of the Michael Snell Literary Agency, whose input inspired the theater theme of the book.

Jim Rue, for his talent in constructing the website, www.take-chargeliving.com as well as for being a caring friend.

Finally, my gratitude to the many clients, who must go unnamed, who have taught me so much over the years. Working with them to help them recast their lives has been the true inspiration for this book.

# *Foreword*

Dr. Marion Jacobs and I worked together for years. We taught classes and workshops as well as supervised and trained graduate students on how to be effective psychotherapists in treating patients/clients at the UCLA Psychology Clinic. One thing I should note before I go any further is that the UCLA Psychology Clinic has been, and justifiably so, continuously rated for years on end as #1 in the nation by the staffs of other clinics coast to coast. This notable honor is due in great part to the hard work, intelligence, and foresight of Marion as Coordinator of the UCLA Clinic for 19 years. These same personal and professional qualities that made her such a good administrator of other scientist/psychologists are embedded in the laudable and important work she has done in this book in showing members of the general public that they indeed do have the built-in ability to take charge of themselves and make significant changes in their lives.

One particular thing I like very much about Marion is her preference for the shorter, more behavioral approaches to change which produce results and useful information for the reader quickly and on a self-transformation basis. Traditional talk psychotherapy can literally take years exploring our underlying, usually poorly and incompletely verbalized beliefs, i.e., those which program our behavior automatically, very often without us correctly thinking about what we are doing and why, including those with erroneously predicted negative outcomes which repeatedly block us from changing things and ourselves for the better. Marion has improved upon this with verbal behavioral methods that quickly lay bare irrelevant and misleading beliefs and teach how to manage the anxiety accompanying these beliefs that slows down our willingness to make changes. Dr. Jacobs methods for dealing with the difficulties in taking charge of our own destiny by effectively making changes is much simpler, faster and can be every bit as effective as traditional talk psychotherapy. What is more, you can do it on your own.

Marion has pulled together a set of methods for making changes work, including such concerns as seeing how well (or not), you're doing now, finding out what continually blocks you from making important changes in your life, and outlining specific goals you want to achieve. Even more importantly she deals with things that can control the limbic mid-brain system, that part of our brain which regulates our emotions and trial and error learning. This is opposed to the upper layers of the cortex which controls our thinking processes, a key to eliminating negative emotion such as fear of changing and anxiety about the whole change process. Our own recidivistic habits and beliefs trigger these negative emotions. They can also be triggered by people who are impacted by the changes you make for the better, and try to resist what you do by attempting to manipulate and intimidate, making you feel guilty, or ignorant for improving yourself. The methods Dr. Jacobs uses to overcome these obstacles and move your life forward are backed by over a hundred years of research, in psychophysiology and neuroscience. Basically what this research tells us is that activation of the upper layers of the cortex will suppress and even eliminate the activation of the limbic system and its emotions of fear and anxiety, particularly what is feared to happen in the future. This is done by having the cortex process information over and over again, especially about the situation that causes anxiety or blocks change. This is basically what Dr. Jacobs does in helping readers ferret out what they fear will happen when changes are made.

Dr. Jacobs has constructed a complete self-help package for dealing with the nasty, self-immobilizing, behavioral/emotional complex of relegating who is in charge of oneself to something or someone outside our persona. Marion has constructed it to go from analysis of the initial problem, through small—but necessary—understandable and achievable steps, through goal attainment and reinforcement of the changes made. A remarkable intellectual and clinical achievement.

This brief note cannot detail all of these steps of change in taking charge of yourself, only recommend you read and follow each of them.

Manuel J. Smith, Ph.D.

Dr. Smith is author of the best-selling self-help book, "When I Say No I Feel Guilty".

# *Introduction: Life Is Not a Dress Rehearsal*

*"You squashed cabbage leaf...you incarnate insult to the English language: I could pass you off as the Queen of Sheba."*

The arrogant language expert, Professor Henry Higgins, boasts this quote to raggedy, screechy Eliza Doolittle, a Cockney flower girl he encounters while waiting for a surprise rainstorm to end. Thus is the opening to Pygmalion, Bernard Shaw's classic play, and My Fair Lady, the smash Broadway musical.

In the ancient myth, the prince Pygmalion sculpts Galatea, a beautiful ivory statue; falls rapturously in love with his own creation; and eventually persuades the goddess Venus to bring Galatea to life in order to become his bride.

Raggedy and poor, but definitely not a statue, the plucky Eliza Doolittle orchestrates her own transformation by turning up at Higgins's residence and persuading him to take her on as his language student. Not reckoning on Eliza's spirit, intelligence, and independence, or on the emotional impact her transformation will have on him, Higgins agrees to her bargain, challenged by a bet with a friend that he can pass her off as high society in six months.

And he does. After months of unrelentingly drilling Eliza in upper-class speech and manners, Higgins triumphantly announces, "By George, she's got it!" The acid test is when he escorts Eliza, now finely mannered, beautifully coiffed, elegantly enunciating, to an embassy gala. The lovely mystery woman wows everyone. The triumph of the evening comes when a prestigious Hungarian linguist stuns the crowd, announcing to the host and hostess that Miss Doolittle is a fraud. Her English is *too* perfect for her to be an English woman. With certainty, he can tell she is not English at all. She is Hungarian. "Not only Hungarian, but of royal blood. She is a princess!"

The story enchants and endures because it taps the transformation yearning we all have to follow our dreams, to become fully alive, and to take charge of our lives. *Take-Charge Living: How to Recast Your Role in Life... One*

*Scene At A Time* acts is a practical guide for how you can make that happen in your own life. In this do-it-yourself version, you star as both Higgins the coach and Eliza the transformed. Better yet, you are Venus, breathing life into your own potential.

If you stop to think about it, change is inevitable. You are not the same person you were twenty, ten, or even five years ago. You are not even exactly the same person you were yesterday. Living day-to-day forces all of us to continually shape and reshape how we think and feel as well as what we believe and do in response to what is happening around us. Take-charge living is about taking charge of that change process instead of allowing external forces to take charge of it for you.

Like Eliza, the power for self-transformation already lies within you. Higgins taught her the facts and coached her through the rehearsals. However, Eliza brought natural potential, a burning desire to improve her life, as well as enough pluck to come to Higgins to ask for help and a willingness to work at it.

If you settle for too little, let others direct your traffic, or daydream about having a better life but do nothing to change the one you have, you are treating this precious time as if it is a warm-up, some kind of dress rehearsal for a real life that is yet to come. Only it's not. For better or worse, this is the one-and-only performance you ever get to give. Doesn't it make sense to cast yourself in a role that moves you toward goals of your own choosing?

Of course it does. However, moving your life in the direction you want it to go almost always means you must make some personal changes. Change takes time and practice. Nature purposely outfitted us to change slowly, mostly in small steps. What a madhouse the world would be if we all walked around changing our thoughts, feelings, and behavior patterns—the very things that give us our personal identity—from moment to moment or even from day to day! Think back to some important way you have changed. Unless it resulted from a trauma, chances are the change came gradually, possibly so gradually you did not even notice you had changed until someone else pointed it out to you.

If your changes are resulting in a happy, fulfilling life, I sincerely congratulate you and encourage you to enjoy them to the utmost. Unless you happen to be interested in knowing more about how those changes happened, you do not need this book. *Take-Charge Living: How to Recast Your Role in Life…One Scene At A Time Acts* is aimed at the person who is living a less than satisfying life but wants to do something about it. If that is you, you will find everything you need for successful personal change in these pages.

To move your life forward, you first need to prepare yourself properly by understanding what is involved in successful change. The first part of the book covers it all, telling you:

- How to set appropriate expectations for how long change will take and what the process will feel like

- How to confront fears of changing

- How to target the right behaviors to change

- How to specify in detail what your new behavior will look like

- How to develop a carefully sequenced practice and feedback plan

- How to deal with emotional resistance to change

Next comes the action phase, where you will get easy-to-follow instructions on how to go step-by-step, putting into action the personal plan for change you have developed. The key is practice, what I typically call dress rehearsals. No actor would face opening night without many, many rehearsals. Well, neither should you! I will teach you how and what to rehearse in the privacy of your home, polishing your performance until you are ready to give your new behavior a tryout in the outside world. Even then, the idea is to work in small steps, to not expect a perfect performance, and to reward yourself for effort. This book gives you everything you need, including how the change process works, guided exercises, lots of encouragement, and the support that comes from reading the real-life stories of others who share your issues.

It's not as if most of us don't know what personal changes we should—and would like to make—to bring greater satisfaction and happiness to our lives. However, reason, intellect, and New Year's resolutions do not come to fruition when confronted with emotions conditioned within us to resist change the minute we move to take action. Those emotions tell us we cannot—or should not—change, the problem is someone else's fault and they should change, or the granddaddy of all excuses for staying stuck, "I'll do it _________(fill in the blank: write that term paper, start my diet, quit vegging, change jobs, look for a mate, see a doctor about the pain, speak up, apply to school, break off this relationship, be on time), as soon as I feel ready."

The reality is that you are not likely to feel ready as you approach the brink of change, precisely because of such inner resistance. If your emotions were not resisting, you would have made the change you desire long ago.

*Take-Charge Living: How to Recast Your Role in Life...One Scene At A Time Acts* directly confronts this reason-versus-emotion dilemma, offering you workable solutions to a problem most self-improvement books either flatly ignore or treat with superficial advice. Unless you have a psychologically sound plan for dealing with emotional resistance to changing yourself, any other efforts you make at self-change are virtually useless.

Let's personalize it: Is there something about you—a way you act, think, or feel—that you would like to change because you know your life would be better if you did? If you answered yes, you are not alone. We are all familiar with that famous winter ritual of making New Year's resolutions. Brimming with enthusiasm, we swear we really will change this year. We will defeat whatever self-defeating behavior we have been indulging in. Our desire to improve is earnest; our intention to change is sincere.

When spring rolls around, why does so little change for so many of those sincere resolution makers? The answer is that the prospect of actually doing what it takes to successfully change arouses hesitancy, doubt, and strong emotional resistance that pull in the opposite direction of sincere intention. Not knowing how to deal with those forces, too many people acknowledge defeat and stick with their old behavior, even though it makes them miserable.

As a clinical psychologist and university professor, I have spent many years helping people successfully change. I know the steps to make it happen. Part of what inspired me to write this book is that my work taught me that people can exert far more control over their moods, feelings, thoughts, and behaviors, (that is, their reactions to life) than they think. What's more, they do not have to go into psychotherapy to do it. Lay-people can make excellent use, on a self-help basis, of the same principles and techniques professionals use to help people take charge of their lives and change. Certainly, some severely distressing situations call for professional help. However, when faced with something we would like to change about ourselves, we can often redirect our life story and make those changes on our own with proper guidance and a road map for how to do it.

Another inspiration for the book comes from some recent and very intriguing research in neuroscience, for example:

- How reason and emotion interact
- How and why we humans interpret things as we do
- Where our resistance to change comes from, even when we know the change would make us happier

I began thinking about how this new, scientifically based knowledge could be usefully applied to helping people change themselves.

Without getting technical, *Take-Charge Living: How to Recast Your Role in Life... One Scene At A Time Acts* connects provocative findings from brain research with the best of my clinical knowledge. The result is a book that explains the dynamics of how people change and offers you, the reader, an easy-to-follow, carefully mapped out, six-act program for overcoming emotional resistance to change and successfully guiding yourself through the change process.

Beyond changing any specific pattern of thinking or behavior, the overarching message of this book is that you can change the whole tenor of your life by adopting what I like to call a take-charge living perspective. That perspective says, as long as more than one way to handle a situation exists, the way you go about it as well as how you think, feel, and act is a choice you are making. Because many of our ways have become so habitual, it may not feel like a choice. But it is.

If the story you are currently playing out on your life's stage is not one you feel like applauding, seriously consider rewriting your script and staging a more satisfying performance. I am here to help with all the necessary support, encouragement, and step-by-step plans for exactly how to do it.

Changing can be an exciting journey. I very much hope you will choose to make that journey with me. We only get one life, so please do not squander yours on endless mental dress rehearsals. The time to move forward is now.

As I wrote this book, I imagined the reader as a friend with whom I want to share some wonderfully exciting things I have learned about personal growth and change. In that spirit, I welcome you to the pages of *Take-Charge Living: How to Recast Your Role in Life... One Scene At A Time Acts.*

Marion K. Jacobs Laguna Beach, California

# PART I
# Star in Your Own Show

*Beginning the Transformation*

# 1

## *Writing the Script*

✦

### *How to Take Charge of Your Life*

Before her automobile accident, co-workers would have described Claudette, a brilliant biologist, not exactly as mean, but definitely aloof, with a supreme self-confidence that bordered on arrogance. Gutsy, a maverick, and a committed loner, Claudette believed in relying on no one except herself. Then that woman plowed broadside into Claudette's Infiniti.

Talk about take-charge living and personal transformation! Claudette spent three months on her back in the ICU, some of it on the critical list. Both her legs and collarbone were broken. Her lung was punctured. A metal halo was screwed into her skull to protect her broken neck. Many more months of painstaking rehabilitation followed. Claudette had no choice except to rely on others, for example, for something as basic as scratching an itchy nose. Her caretakers—doctors, nurses, aides, and therapists—were wonderful, every one of them.

Claudette was initially bitter. However, over time, she not only reevaluated just her current situation, but she looked at her whole approach to life. Her usual one-woman act could not work here. Survival and sanity depended upon collaboration with the entire cast. That meant communicating, accepting help under the most trying, life-threatening conditions, taking direction, and eventually even reaching out to other patients. Maybe her one-woman act was not the best way under any circumstances. A changed woman emerged from University Hospital, a person newly aware of her own need for connection with others.

Although many of us never face challenges of that magnitude, our survival, like Claudette's, demands that we change, adjust our thinking and our behavior to respond to the continually changing conditions around us. While changing may be inevitable, how you change, that is, being in charge of what you do (what I call take-charge living) is anything but inevitable. Take-charge living requires self-awareness, concentration, and determination.

Take a quick take-charge living check on yourself by asking yourself which of these two statements is more true about you:

1. I have been in charge of most of the decisions that have shaped my life and myself.

2. I have mostly allowed other people and external circumstances to shape my life for me.

If the second statement is you, don't be discouraged. This book is all about how to change that. Fortunately, we are all capable of exerting far more control over our moods, feelings, thoughts, and behaviors (that is, our reactions to life) than many of us think. Coping effectively in life is not a matter of luck, having the best genes, or wealth, even though those are certainly nice things to have. Coping effectively is a matter of learning the steps to take to consciously and purposefully take charge of our lives.

Even when confronted with some of life's most painful situations (the death of a loved one, unwanted divorce, job layoffs, physical and mental abuse, natural disasters, chronic and terminal illnesses), there are ways of taking charge and coping that work—even make us grow—and ways of coping that drag us deeper into misery.

Nancy and Helen were both diagnosed with breast cancer. Nancy sank into a deep depression. When her family urged her to get a second opinion before deciding on treatment, she waved them away.

"I trust the doctor," she said.

When they tried getting her to do anything pleasurable, like go to a movie, she refused. In fact, Nancy barely left the couch. Her helpless answer to everything was that there was no point.

"It's God's way," she said.

Nancy's emotional bond to the idea she couldn't do anything to help herself made facing cancer so much harder. Not only did her insistence on her own helplessness drag her down, it dragged the rest of the family down with her, effectively rendering everyone helpless. Only Nancy was wrong. This wasn't God's way. It was Nancy's way. Sadly, it was Nancy's very mistaken way.

Helen was just the opposite. She strode through her front door after her doctor gave her the diagnosis, logged onto the Internet, and read everything she could find about her specific type of cancer. Then she went to chat rooms. The patients she talked with impressed on her how important it was that she understand the different medical choices available to her and get independent consultations before settling on a doctor and treatment. They also urged her to join a breast cancer support group, which she did. Now, five months posttreatment, Helen's spirits are good. She is actively raising funds for cancer research. That is not to say Helen, just like Nancy, did not go through some terrible bouts of fear and stress. The difference was Helen's determination to fight back by taking action, including educating herself, making good decisions, and doing everything possible to keep her spirits up.

Research shows that people like Helen, who take action on their own behalf, not only have a better quality of life, but they actually do better medically than those who succumb to passivity, pessimism, and helplessness. In fact, some evidence suggests cancer patients with a "fighting spirit" may live longer. That's a pretty wild idea when you stop and think about it. A take-charge attitude can positively impact disease and possibly even prolong life! How does that happen?

Little by little, neuroscience research is filling in answers to that very complex question. One fascinating finding is how closely our moods and emotions, thoughts and behaviors, and immune and other bodily systems are all connected to one another. They are not only connected; all heavily influence one another. This mind-body knowledge empowers us. By understanding how we are wired together, we can better figure out what we need to do to reshape aspects of ourselves we want to change.

Wouldn't we be foolish if we didn't take advantage of what science and clinical experience can teach us about how to take control of our lives and stop giving our power away to forces outside ourselves? That is exactly what this book does. It provides you with the opportunity to start writing your own script for your life and learn to change in ways that work best for you. This book is the practical self-help guide for exactly how to do it, the most empowering gift you can give yourself.

Let's personalize things: How well do you meet the challenge of changing your behavior when you know it would improve the quality of your life? To help you answer that question, look at the following scale. Picture number 1 as people who feel quite helpless, almost totally out of control of their lives. Number 10 is the opposite, people who feel on top of things and quite in charge of their lives. Most of us fall somewhere in between.

Take a moment. Think about it. At this point in your life, where do you place yourself?

How Much I Feel In Control Of My Life

| 1 | 2 | 3 | 4 | 5 | 6 | 7 | 8 | 9 | 10 |
|---|---|---|---|---|---|---|---|---|---|
| I feel very little personal control over my life. | | | | | | | | | I feel a lot of personal control over over my life. |

Chances are, the less personal control (that is, the less in charge you feel over your life), the less happy you are. As a clinical psychologist, I've spent many years working with many different kinds of people dealing with many different kinds of problems. I am convinced the bottom line is this:

- Feeling you have a reasonable degree of personal control over your life is essential to your emotional health and well-being.

- Research shows a sense of personal control over your life is also a major contributor to keeping you physically healthy.

- The opposite is true as well. Feeling helpless is bad for both your mental and physical health.

The scale above is a useful first step for taking stock of your situation. Now let me ask you this: Are you reasonably satisfied with how you run your life? I don't mean, "Does life always treat you well?" Of course it doesn't. But do you mostly like—perhaps I should also say respect—the attitudes you carry with you toward people and situations as well as the way you handle yourself personally? How you cope with problems? If your answers are more negative than positive, the guidelines in this book can help you change.

As a next step, ask yourself, "Am I willing to do something to change?" You don't have to know what that something is. You do not even have to feel like changing. You just must be willing to do try it. It's my job to show you the path and guide you as long as you are willing to take that walk with me. Take-charge living is a gift that only you have the power to give to yourself. Yes, it takes some effort, but not an overwhelming amount. The guidelines in these pages will offer you support and show you exactly what to do. I can promise you this: Making the effort to learn how to live a take-charge life is worth the payoff. It is a gift to yourself that keeps on giving.

Phyllis is a woman I met when I first started writing this book. She is fifty-nine years old, sincere, hardworking, loving, and deeply religious. She has spent the past two plus years coping with several changes she never planned. Her marriage broke up. She moved to California from the Midwest. She is trying to restart her painting and housecleaning business while exploring a totally new lifestyle. I asked Phyllis to be my "woman on the street." Would she give me some feedback about my plans for this book? She was delighted.

"What do you think?" I asked after she had read the opening pages. "Would you buy the book?"

"I absolutely would," Phyllis said in her lovely Chicago accent.

"Why?" I asked. "What about it interests you?"

"Well," she answered thoughtfully, "you've said a lot to me in a few pages. I especially liked the rating scale. I've been through a lot of personal changes. I know what it is like not to be able to get out of bed and to lie there crying for days on end. I've been on Prozac. I've had professional help. I've grown from it all. Overall, I'm doing pretty well. Some days are better than others. If I can get just one new tool from your book that helps me cope, it would be worth reading just for that. Just one new tool."

"Wow," I thought, "just one new tool, and she'll be happy?" That's easy. But these pages offer lots more than that to help you get your show on the road.

## The Take-Charge Living Perspective

Think of take-charge living as both an attitude you adopt and a pledge you make to yourself. Once made, you always carry that attitude/pledge around with you, calling on it many times in the course of a day to remind yourself how you promised yourself you intend to approach life. The heart of the pledge is accepting the fact that, regardless of what situation you face (trivial/major or commonplace/ rare), you have choices about how you are going to respond to it. Take-charge living begins with accepting responsibility for that fact.

Do you even buy the idea that, in whatever situation you find yourself, what you do and how you respond to people and events is always a choice you are making? It is not necessarily a conscious choice, especially if it is something you have done the same way time and again, but it is a choice nonetheless. As long as more than one way exists for a person to respond in that situation, the way you actually respond is your choice.

Even choosing to do nothing is a choice. As is true with all choices, choosing to do nothing affects how things work out. You might say doing nothing is the ultimate passive choice.

In contrast are all kinds of aggressive choices. I know a guy named Mike with a really short fuse about many things. His pet peeve is drivers who cut ahead of him on the freeway, even though Mike himself does it all the time. One time, Mike worked himself up into such a rage that he purposely rammed into another man's car. Mike honestly believes, when he feels his anger go past a certain point, it means it is beyond his control. He has no choice except lashing out.

"Nonsense," you say. "Nobody has to ram somebody else's car!"

Of course, it's nonsense. That is precisely my point. Mike can tell himself whatever he wants, but he is choosing to act aggressively, whether he believes it or not.

You are probably thinking, "Okay, Mike has choices in those situations. What about the times in life when we are faced with events beyond our control? You can't control other people. What they say, think, do can sometimes be very hurtful. You can't stop a fire, flood, tornado, or earthquake from turning your life inside out. You can't fend off kidney failure or heart disease."

This is all true. We cannot control other people. Thinking we can is more illusion than reality. Many times, we have no control over events, certainly not a fire, flood, or quake. But (and this is a big "but"), we can control how we respond to those people and events.

Let's personalize the discussion: Would your life benefit from a little more take-charge living? Think about your relationships with other people, including friends, spouse or partner, your children, family, coworkers, neighbors, doctors, store clerks, or whomever. For the most part, are you satisfied with how you interact with them and how you respond to the things they say or do? If so, that's great. I really mean it. It is great to feel good about yourself and your relationships.

Unfortunately, many people do not. They feel pushed around. They feel others take advantage of them. They are afraid to speak up and honestly express an opinion. Alternatively, they talk too much and listen very little but do not understand why they have no friends. Some lose out on relationships because they take everything too personally or get defensive. Others are approval junkies, forever seeking reassurance they are okay. Many people are aware of their bad habits, even though they may not do anything about them. Even those who are oblivious to their role in messing up relationships often sense their life is not what it could be.

The need for more take-charge living may not be primarily about relationships at all. Imagine, for example, you have the misfortune to be hit by a natural disaster such as a mudslide, flood, or earthquake. How are you likely to react? I mean, are you take-charge in the sense of being resourceful? Do you handle things constructively? Would you be able to provide comfort, guidance, and support to yourself and your loved ones? Or are you more likely to feel helpless and immobilized, or enraged, or turn to drugs or alcohol to get away from your troubles?

For some, the take-charge living challenge is neither dealing with bad relationships nor stressful events. Rather, it is mustering the courage to think creatively, tackle new projects, and open up to positive opportunity when faced by the unexpected, unfamiliar, or unwanted.

In the next chapter, I will ask you to complete a couple of personal checklists to help you take stock of how take-charge you are in running your life. Seeing your current patterns clearly lets you pinpoint which things satisfy you and which you would like to change.

# 2

## *Preparing for the Stage*

✦

### *How to Measure Your Current Performance*

We'll use two checklists to audition you and your scripts. Chances are, you are happier with how you respond in some situations than others. Most of us cope better in some areas than others. The following checklists were designed to help you pinpoint for yourself where things are going fine (and please remember to give yourself credit for that) and where you think you could benefit from making changes.

The goal is to get you thinking in specific terms, that is, to systematically take stock of how confident, in control, and satisfied you feel with particular ways you behave toward specific types of people in specific types of situations. Note that the focus is on you and only you. That is important to get clear.

Mary is becoming increasingly disenchanted and angry with Tyler, her live-in boyfriend. Tyler, a slob, insists on having the last word about everything and does not care about anyone else's feelings. Mary is tired of arguing, and she's tired of sulking. When asked what she wants to do about it, instead of considering a rewrite of her own script in their relationship, Mary's answer to the problem is for Tyler to rewrite his.

"I want him to grow up! His mother was still buttering his toast when he was twenty-one. Now he thinks all women are there to serve him. Well, dammit, I have needs, too. He's got to start changing!"

As with so many other people, Mary believes in fixing her problem by having somebody else do the changing. But what if Tyler won't change? Up to now, despite her complaining, he has not. Like the rest of us, Mary really only has control over one person, and that person is Mary. Trying to control others is an illusion. The real question is: What does she need to do differently to get her life unstuck? Maybe it involves communicating differently with Tyler. Maybe it involves a decision to leave the relationship. Whatever the answer, it's Mary who has to take action and do something different from what she is doing now.

This chapter is about you changing yourself. Keeping that solidly in mind, let's continue with a reading of the roles you've written for yourself.

## Checklist 1: My Relationship Roles

Other people are an important part of our lives. Let's take a look at how you are doing in relating to them when it comes to:

- Openness and independence
- Understanding others
- Communicating with others
- Expressing emotions effectively
- Thinking constructively
- Faith in your ability to cope (sometimes called self-efficacy) For each of these six areas, you have three choices:
    - ➢ Read the choices carefully. Think honestly how they apply to you.
    - ➢ Check either A, B, or C, whichever choice comes closest to describing you best.
    - ➢ At the end of each set of questions, it asks: Who? (For now, leave that blank.)

## Openness and Independence

Do you act on your own? Do you act wisely?

A. I learn from others, but I then make up my own mind what to think or do.

B. I let other people influence how I think and act too much of the time.

C. I don't let other people influence me enough of the time.

Who?

## Understanding Others

How well do you tune in to other people? How well do you balance that with expressing yourself?

A. I am good at tuning in to how others feel, but I also know how to express my own feelings effectively.

B. I express myself. I am not terribly interested in how others feel.

C. I pay attention to how others feel, often to the neglect of saying how I feel.

Who?

## Communicating with Others

How effectively do you express your views as well as listen and understand other people?

A. I am open and honest. I do not apologize for my ideas. I also listen carefully to others and try to understand their views, even if I do not agree with them. I know how to find a good balance between speaking and listening. When I talk with others, I treat them respectfully. I make good eye contact. My tone of voice is good, and I come across as poised.

B. I tend to be fearful of speaking up honestly or sometimes of speaking up at all. When I do talk, I tend to come across as uncertain. Other people sense they can overpower the discussion with their point of view.

C. I speak up. I am talkative. I like controlling a conversation. I press others to agree with my views. I do not mind interrupting others if I think what I have to say is more important. I can be impatient because I often think my ideas are better.

Who?

## Expressing Emotions Effectively

Does your way of expressing your emotions help you or hinder you in communicating with others?

A. I am not overly emotional nor am I overly bland when I talk. I know how to express my feelings in a way that helps me get across what I have to say in a constructive way.

B. I tend to overreact and express too much emotion, for example, talk or joke too much; be hostile, argumentative, aggressive or assaultive, silly, loud, or too intense; or get aroused and upset too easily.

C. I tend to do one or both of the following:

- Hold back what I am thinking and feeling, for example, being too quiet or physically tense, not revealing anything personal, showing no reactions, or reacting in a way that is hard to read, *and/or*

- Be too accepting, smile too much, or put on a cheerful face, even when it does not fit the situation or is not my true feeling.

Who?

## Thinking Constructively

Do you think constructively under both positive and negative conditions?

A. I am generally optimistic. I try looking on the bright side of things. Overall, I enjoy relationships, my life, and myself. When bad events happen, I view them as temporary challenges or obstacles that can be overcome. I see defeat as a temporary setback, a reason to work harder. I do not engage in a lot of self-blame.

B. I tend to be overly critical of others or myself. (This can take different forms, for example, being cynical, sarcastic, rejecting, aggressive, unpleasant, faultfinding, or uncomplimentary.)

C. I tend to feel helpless or unassertive. I imagine the worst and/or give up easily.

Who?

## Faith in Your Ability to Cope with Most Situations

This is sometimes called a sense of self-efficacy.

A. I know how to size up situations well. I trust in my own abilities and capacity to solve problems. I take the initiative to do so. I know how locate the resources if I need help.

B. I doubt my ability to make decisions and take effective action. I do not take action when I should, or I seek excessive reassurance from others first. I do not pursue my own goals enough.

C. Too often, I think I can handle things better than I really can. I tend to ignore or make light of the talents of others.

Who?

## How to Analyze Your Results

If you chose A, it means you are doing fine in that area. If you chose B or C, it means you have room for change. Please look at the list of different relationships below:

- Friends
- Intimates (spouse, partner, lover, and so forth)
- Adult family members
- Children
- Authority figures
- Business contacts
- People I work with (boss, coworkers, colleagues, subordinates)
- Casual acquaintances
- Strangers

For any area in which you answered B or C, at the end of the question, where it says "Who?" write which kind of relationship or the name of a specific person this concern applies to.

## Example: Question #5—Thinking Constructively

Let's say you answered C, meaning you tend to feel helpless or unassertive and give up easily. Chances are that for you it is more of a problem with some people than others. Maybe it is a problem only with one specific person.

Perhaps you are fine at home and with friends, but you lack confidence at work. In that case, you would write "People I work with" after "Who?" On the other hand, if only your boss intimidates you at work and not most people, you would write "My boss" or the boss's name.

This completes the survey of how take-charge you are in relation to other people. In a later chapter, I will ask you to pick one of these problem areas for practice in learning the take-charge living approach.

To round out the picture of your current life scripts you act upon, let's also survey your take-charge living habits in relation to yourself. The following mini-survey provides a snapshot of that.

## Checklist 2: My Role with Myself

1. Do you neglect or poorly manage any of the following?
    - Your health? Yes______ No_______
    - Your body? Yes______ No_______
    - Your possessions? Yes______ No_______
    - Your living space? Yes______ No_______
    - Your finances? Yes______ No_______
    - Your time? Yes______ No_______
    - Other? ____________________

2. Do you abuse food, alcohol, or drugs? Do you smoke? Do you engage in any other risky, detrimental, or personally harmful behaviors?
    Yes______ No_______

3. Do you lose out because you procrastinate about things that are important to you?
    Yes______ No_______

4. Do you avoid pursuing your life goals? Yes______ No_______

5. Other problem areas? ______________________________________

A yes answer to any of these questions points out you are not in good enough charge when it comes to taking care of yourself.

Taking charge of your relationship to yourself is every bit as important as your relationships with others. The principles of take-charge living I will be discussing in the upcoming sections of the book apply equally well, whether we are talking about relating to others or yourself.

These two surveys you just completed are an important first step in applying a take-charge living approach. Precisely spelling out where you have problems—either with other people or yourself—lets you know precisely where you need to direct your efforts at changing. If more than one problem area showed up, I will ask you to work on only one at a time when we begin rehearsing. From years of experience, I know that staying focused (that is, working on one target behavior at a time) is the most effective strategy for getting good results. More than one and it is too easy to lose focus and get confused and discouraged.

With your personal surveys completed, we're ready to go forward. In the next chapter, you will learn the secret to successfully changing your behavior. After that, we move you to planning and implementing your first personal change. But please keep in mind that adopting a take-charge living attitude and making personal changes is not a matter of instant insights and quick fixes. Quite the opposite. It is a process of understanding principles, putting those principles into practice, seeing how it goes, fine-tuning your efforts, and then practicing some more. There is nothing magical about it. You followed the same steps when you learned physical skills like riding a bike, swimming, or driving a car. Learning those things took time and practice too.

It also helps if you don't keep telling yourself that making a change will be scary, loathsome, or some other negative big deal…not that trying to change something about yourself might not feel scary or loathsome when you first think about doing it. But what good does it do to keep rehearsing that idea? About as much as sticking your tongue in a hole in your tooth where a filling fell out. It does not fix the tooth, but it sure roughs up your tongue!

Instead, have a little fun with the following exercise. Even though it is just an exercise, it gives you a taste of what it is like to put distance between yourself and unhelpful ideas. It also gives you a bit of practice in generating helpful mental images. Imagery, as I will show you later, is an important skill when learning how to live the take-charge life.

Here's the exercise. Picture your negative feelings or any other resistances to changing yourself as so many pieces of dirty laundry scattered on the floor of your mind. Imagine yourself gathering those feelings together in a bundle, extracting the bundle from inside your head, and putting it in a box with a lid on a shelf in the far corner of the room. Store the bundle there for a while.

Now, with your mind freed from doubts, crank up your imagination. Imagine learning to take charge of your life and orchestrating personal change—not as an impossibility or even a chore—as an adventure! Pretend you are a trained scientist. Trying the take-charge living approach is an experiment you are going to run on yourself in your personal laboratory of life. Like any good scientist, you cannot sit in your armchair and decide just by thinking about whether take-charge living will work for you. No, of course not! You must put take-charge living to the test, that is, actually try it and then observe what happens. Think of the two of us as embarking on a scientific journey together with me as your guide.

In that spirit of adventure and scientific inquiry, we will take your show on the road. The journey will be easier if you accept and adopt the following five principles:

### The change process focuses on you, not other people.

As long as there is more than one way you could respond to a given situation, you work on changing what you are doing if you are not satisfied with the results from your current ways.

Ask yourself, "Is what I am doing working for me? Am I moving toward—not away from—my goals?" If your answer is no, ask yourself the next question, "What do I need to change in my thinking or behavior to turn things around?"

Note, take-charge living does not involve spending your energy wishing, blaming, maneuvering, or demanding that others change.

### Feelings are not always your friends.

Feelings can be your friends, but they can also be your enemy. Knowing when to follow your feelings and when to say "no thanks" to them is critical. One of the most important things this book teaches is not only how to understand the connection between reason and emotions, but more importantly, what to do when reason and emotions (feelings) pull you in opposite directions.

### What is learned can be unlearned. Something better can be put in its place.

Much of how we think, act, and feel has been learned. That's bad news if you don't like the results you're getting. But bad learning is only a bad habit.

You can break that habit by learning better ways of doing things to put in its place.

**Having appropriate expectations about how change occurs is essential.**

Change rarely happens all at once. It is usually step-by-step, sometimes in baby steps. Changing yourself means practicing something new, evaluating how you're doing, fine-tuning your responses, and practicing some more. Change takes time and patience. Please expect that. Also, don't be a perfectionist. Give yourself a pat on the back for making an effort. Then keep practicing and fine-tuning your performance. **At its best, take-charge living is a dynamic approach to living for the rest of your life.**

That sounds good, but what does it really mean? First and foremost, it means taking active responsibility for charting the course of your life. It also means understanding the world is forever changing, so, as a matter of course, you expect to change as well. Dynamic living also means:

- Learning to rely on your own judgment
- Not making a habit of negative thinking
- Treating problems as challenges to be solved

The research is clear. People living a take-charge life not only feel better, but they look better, enjoy better health, and even live longer under some conditions. What are we waiting for? Let's get some of that for you!

# 3

## *Staging a Hit*

✦

### *How to Temper Your Emotions with Reason*

Reasoning is critical to your successful functioning. Solving problems and making decisions depends on it. However, reasoning needs steady input from your physical and emotional systems to function properly. Far from sound decisions being a matter of reason versus emotion (as so many people think), living effectively, maintaining good relationships, pursuing your life's goals, and even managing adversity depend upon reason and emotion working cooperatively. As we all know too well, they sometimes do just the opposite.

The secret to staging a hit for your life's performance is knowing how to manage the situation when your common sense and feelings are pulling you in opposite directions. You cannot wish away feelings that are getting in your way. However, you definitely can do some things to override their power to control you. I will state the secret briefly and then spend lots of time explaining what I mean. Even though it sounds simple, making it happen is not. When your feelings keep you from going into action to make changes you know would make your life happier, the secret to success lies in learning how to tolerate those feelings without following their dictates. That's a tall order, given how insistent and compelling feelings can be and how powerfully they can push people around. Once you master the techniques this book will teach you, managing those negative feelings to get your show on the road becomes a lot easier.

In this chapter, I spend time discussing the mind-body connection, focusing particularly on how reason and emotion interact with one another and what impact that has on you. The more you understand about what is going on inside you, the easier you will find it to tolerate negative feelings that resist change and move yourself forward anyway. Happily, as you get better and better at doing that, the negative feelings themselves diminish.

After all, most sane, reasonable people want to be in charge of their lives. We all know that thinking positively, acting capably (that is, directing our own show) simply feels better. Why then are so many seemingly sane, reasonable people willing to let other people and circumstances control their lives? And even when they feel intense dissatisfaction with how things are going, how is it that they feel so helpless to change things? They would like to dump their script and get a new one. Their helplessness comes from listening to their feelings, feelings that are telling them the part they are now playing is the only one they will ever be able to play.

My neighbor Marv is a classic case of misery married to inaction. Looking for answers, Marv reads advice to the lovelorn columns, his horoscope, and an occasional self-help book. Year after year, he remains stuck in his lonely, unhappy life. An attractive professional man in his mid-fifties, Marv is currently in the process of cleaning up the remains of his fourth failed marriage. He will be the first to admit this latest broken relationship is not a random event. A charming, sincere, and well-spoken man, Marv has no trouble attracting women, but remains clueless why his intimate relationships ultimately never work out.

Once, when he dropped in for a cup of coffee and began complaining about his trouble with women, I asked if he wanted to change that.

With an obvious lack of enthusiasm, Marv answered, "It depends what it takes. I'm not interested in any deep psychotherapy."

I said it would not have to take deep psychotherapy. Marv did not bother to ask me what it would take. Why? From Marv's perspective, changing how he relates to women looms as too stressful. In fact, Marv sees it is an impossible undertaking. When Marv pictures himself holed up in his condominium, watching TV, and drinking gin and tonic all night (which is what he does most nights), and then pictures himself trying to work on bettering his relationships with women when he does not really have the foggiest idea how to go about it, what do you suppose Marv's feelings tell him to do? Of course, what feels comfortable and safe! What's that? Remain holed up, continue to feel lonely, drink away the pain, and ignore that he is becoming an alcoholic. Being holed up, lonely, and alcoholic, he at least avoids the profound anxiety and deep sense of personal failure he has come to associate with romantic relationships.

Nobody can afford Marv's kind of safety. Often, the alternative means making changes we do not feel energized to make. This book will show you how to get going with whatever personal changes you deem to be in your best interest, even if you do not feel like doing it. Learning when and how to not follow your feelings, regardless of how compelling they are (and feelings are nothing if not compelling), is one of the most important things this book teaches.

Too many psychotherapists do not pay adequate attention to this issue. They help clients gain insight into their problems and help them spell out new ways to act, sometimes even role-playing proposed new behaviors. However, when these clients go into the real world (they sometimes merely have to think of going into the real world) to try these new behaviors, they are often unprepared to deal with the flood of negative feelings and resistance to taking action that is likely to occur.

Insight into a problem along with a picture of how you want to behave is rarely enough. Doing what you think is best can be painfully difficult if your feelings are resisting. It is so difficult that some people then throw in the towel on changing. There are ways to deal with that difficulty. If we want to change, besides insight and an outline of new behaviors, we need a strategy for handling the powerful negative feelings and resistance that almost inevitably arise when we try changing something about ourselves. Learning how to move ahead, despite emotional resistance, is the secret to staging your own successful take-charge living show. The foundation for that strategy requires understanding the following points, about which I will have lots more to say as we proceed on our journey.

1. Reason, emotion, bodily reactions, and behavior are inseparably intertwined. They influence each other every instant, awake or asleep. This tight connection and nonstop cross talk is part of the natural survival system of humans, both as individuals and a species.

2. We are often unaware of how our reason, physiology, emotions, and behavior impact each other because much of it occurs below the level of our conscious awareness.

3. When all four systems (reason, emotions, bodily reactions, and behavioral action tendencies) are moving in concert, we experience a sense of unity, consistency, and a sense of direction. When logic pulls one way and feelings pull another, we experience turmoil, conflict, and uncertainty about how to act.

Take-charge living requires knowing how to make these complex systems work for—instead of against—you. To accomplish that, in coming chapters you will be learning:

- How the mind-body connection is impacted by constant cross talk among thoughts, feelings, bodily sensations, and behavior

- How to tune in to those thoughts, feelings, bodily sensations, and action tendencies, especially when they conflict with one another

- How to modify those thoughts, feelings, bodily sensations, and action tendencies when conflict amongst them prevents you from pursuing your goals

- How to manage negative feelings that resist change, freeing you up to take whatever actions you deem to be in your best interests

As you learn these skills step-by-step, your self-awareness will blossom, and confidence in your powers of personal control will deepen.

## Reason and Emotion—Married For Life

Some recent neuroscience research findings are helpful. They tell us a lot about the nature, power, and importance of the mind-body interplay. The more we understand how this works, the more power it gives us to orchestrate changes within ourselves.

I will begin with a quote I like very much from the introduction of Dr. Antonio Damasio's book, *Descartes Error: Emotion, Reason, and the Human Brain*:

> *I had been advised early in life that sound decisions came from a cool head, that emotions and reason did not mix any more than oil and water. I had grown up accustomed to thinking that the mechanisms of reason existed in a separate province of the mind, where emotion should not be allowed to intrude, and when I thought of the brain behind that mind, I envisioned separate neural systems for reason and emotion.*[1]

Dr. Damasio's words capture what many of us were raised to believe. Reason, logic, and rationality are the bedrock of sensible life planning. Emotions, moods, and feelings only sidetrack us from common sense and solid decision-making. Reason versus emotion (opposites) is an obvious division as easy to grasp as black versus white or up versus down.

---

1 Antonio Damasio, Descartes' Error: Emotion, Reason, and the Human Brain. (New York: Penguin Books, 1994), xv.

Alas, some clever scientists have recently started proving it is not true. In fact, quite the opposite is true. As they unfold the fascinating picture of how we human beings are internally constructed, these neuroscientists are demonstrating very complex, tightly woven connections and communication between reason and emotion. Reason and emotion turn out to be married for life. Our challenge is making it a happy marriage.

Only an expert in neuroscience could fully explain all that is understood so far about the relationships among mind, body, and brain and, within that, the connections among reason, emotion, and behavior. Even the experts admit we are dealing with an unimaginably complex jigsaw puzzle.

While new information keeps coming, many pieces of the puzzle are still missing.

With our limited time on earth, you and I cannot wait for all the answers. We need to figure out how to live the best life we can right now. I am personally committed to doing that. As a clinical psychologist, I am committed to helping others do it as well. Let's begin examining this newly emerging understanding of the reason-emotion connection in people with a focus on how such information can help us do a first-rate job of running our own lives.

As humans, our most basic task is bodily survival—not thinking, pleasure, or conversation. Just pure bodily survival. Unless our bodies survive, our genes cannot be passed to future generations, which, in effect, dooms us to extinction. So obviously, if body survival doesn't come first, nothing else really matters.

But stop and think what bodily survival actually entails. The body, with all its complicated systems, must constantly regulate itself internally. At the same time, it must ward off danger and sustain itself through moment-to-moment communication with the external world. High among its priorities is a need for rapid responses to possible threat. But simply hiding from or warding off danger isn't enough. Our survival also requires we grow by exploring novel situations in the world around us. That's how we learn to distinguish things that are a potential value to us and things that are a potential threat. What kind of mind-body arrangement could possibly accomplish all that? A mind-body arrangement that allows for many continuous high-speed communications.

This, of course, is exactly how we are wired. Under normal conditions, asleep or awake, high-speed processing of signals within the body's systems and among the parts of the brain as well as between the body and brain keeps us alive and hopefully thriving.

Another requirement for survival is a signal system that allows emotion and reason to cross talk, that is, to share the images stored in our minds and bodies that represent past learning and experience, present input, and future plans as well as contribute to our sense of who we are. Without such signaling, we would not have the information we need to solve problems and make the endless string of small and big decisions that comprise living.

Think of the many minor decisions we make in a day. Shall I stay in bed five more minutes or not? Would I rather have Cheerios or scrambled eggs for breakfast? What should I wear to work? Add to that life's ongoing major decisions like having a baby, choosing or leaving a mate, starting a business, dropping out of school, joining the military, taking drugs, picking a career. All day and every day, survival demands problem-solving and decision-making.

In his fascinating book, *The Developing Mind*, Dr. Daniel J. Siegel notes the brain has an estimated 100 billion neurons, which would extend for two million miles if stretched out. Each of these neurons averages 10,000 direct connections to other neurons. All together, we are talking about one million billion connections, making the brain the most complex structure on earth. Dr. Siegel points out that it takes a healthy integration of all this complexity to give us a coherent, narrative picture of ourselves over time.[2]

The important news (in many ways the new news from the researchers) is that successful problem-solving and decision-making, far from strictly a matter of cool-headed rationality, rests on an intricate, delicately balanced interaction between feelings and thoughts. If the areas of your brain governing emotion are damaged, regardless of how intact your cognitive (thinking) system remains, your ability to reason, make decisions, and function in society would be seriously impaired.

That's precisely what happened to Phineas P. Gage, a handsome, bright, extremely capable young man of twenty-five.[3] In 1848, Gage was bossing a group of railroad workers laying new tracks across Vermont. Gage was normally a master at preparing high explosive detonations. This time, an unfortunate distraction caused Gage to pound his crafted iron rod into the hole in the rock containing both explosive powder and fuse before his helper had carried out Gage's order to pour in the necessary sand covering. Boom! There was a deafening explosion, and the iron bar (weighing more than thirteen pounds and nearly four feet long and one-and-a-quarter inches in diameter) entered at Gage's left cheek, pierced the base of his skull, traveled across the front of his brain, and sailed out through the top of his head. Almost as amazing as Gage's survival was the fact he remained conscious and coherent. He could walk and talk immediately after the accident.

---

2 Daniel J. Siegel, The Developing Mind: Toward a Neurobiology of Interpersonal Experience (New York: Guilford Press, 1999), 13.

3 For a detailed, excitingly narrated account, see Dr. Damasio's book.

Following a period of infection, Phineas Gage, even though doctors declared him physically recovered, was a man with an indelibly altered personality.

Before the accident, Gage was a temperate, energetic, shrewd, persistent person. He was very capable of carrying out his plans effectively. The post-trauma Gage had morphed into a foul-mouthed, intemperate boozing brawler. He was obstinate and unable to follow through with plans or hold a job for long. He utterly lacked in concern for others or his own future. Dr. Damasio reports this story of Gage, along with research on his own patients suffering related types of brain damage, to underscore how much reason and emotion are intricately connected and interdependent: Dr. Damasio states:

> *In short, there appears to be a collection of systems in the human brain dedicated to the goal-oriented thinking process we call reasoning, and to the response selection we call decision making, with a special emphasis on the personal and social domain. This same collection of systems is also involved in emotion and feeling, and is partly dedicated to processing body signals.*[4]

Reason, emotion, and bodily signals are intimately interconnected, but that does not mean they are always working together in joyful harmony. Jenna is a classic case of reason and emotion not cooperating.

Jenna is a bright, delightful, attractive young woman of twenty-six who has yet to arrive at an appointment on time. Whether it's meeting a friend, a session with a client (Jenna is a personal physical fitness trainer who makes house calls), or arriving at the beauty salon to have her hair done, it's money in the bank that Jenna will be ten to thirty minutes late. Fortunately, she is very likeable. Otherwise, nobody would bother with her at all. But by running late most of the time she's lost clients, lost new referrals, ticked off friends and stresses herself silly.

Jenna is well aware of the negative impact of her behavior, that is, the disorganization that comes from dashing out at the last minute, weaving dangerously through traffic while dreaming up excuses, and, worst of all, facing the anger and sarcasm that confronts her when she finally arrives at her destination. Unsurprisingly, Jenna's self-esteem is low, and her stomach is usually knotted.

Why doesn't Jenna use logic or reason (call it plain old common sense) and tell herself to plan better, get up earlier, or do whatever it takes to be on

---

4 Antonio Damasio, Descartes' Error, 32.

time and quit damaging her life? Of course, Jenna does. She lectures herself all the time. It adds to her stress, but it doesn't help her change her behavior. And that's the heart of the matter. Why doesn't she simply force herself to be on time, knowing how much easier, happier, and less stressful her life would be if she did?

Instead of trying to answer the question about Jenna, it might be more useful to turn the question on yourself. Do you have some area of your life in which you know you would be better off if you changed your behavior? If so, why don't you just do it? The answer lies with your emotions, that is, how you feel. When you think about changing (let's say speaking up more, not procrastinating on projects, confronting some issue in your marriage that has been eating at you for a long time, or seeing the doctor about unexplained bleeding), when you picture what it would be like to deal with the problem head on, you get a bad feeling. In essence, that bad feeling is telling your brain if you go ahead (that is, you take action, which, in your heart, you wish you could and logically know you should), then you are in for a painful or dangerous experience.

Maybe you are one of those people whose problem is not avoiding action. Instead, you overreact when you know it is not in your best interests to do so. What is the benefit of telling off your boss instead of calmly discussing grievances; abusing food, booze, or drugs; dealing abusively with your kids; trying to one-up others in conversation; giving unwanted advice; or insisting things be done your way all the time?

We harm ourselves by overdoing things for the same reason we harm ourselves by avoiding doing other things. It is a fear of a painful experience. That is sometimes easier to see when we're avoiding something. For instance, you may avoid the doctor when there is blood in your stool. Most likely, that is a fear of hearing you have a serious illness. The opposite of avoidance, overindulgence (or "acting out" as some call it), can also be seen as a fear of pain. The pain in this case is the physical and emotional discomfort of not yielding to strong urges, for example, the urge to overeat, drink too much, have the last word, push unwanted sex, or lose your temper.

We usually don't think in terms of deciding to act or not act. As situations arise, we just do what feels right, what we are used to doing, or what our feelings make us think is our only choice to do. That works just fine most of the time. Practically speaking, there are so many choice points in the course of any day that we need to do things fairly automatically (as opposed to consciously) or we would be hopelessly bogged down before we even made it out of bed.

That's because stored inside you are millions (more likely trillions or zillions) of feelings, ideas, images, thoughts, beliefs, expectations, and action tendencies that have been accumulating since infancy or maybe even since the womb. Through your life's experiences year in and year out, you continue adding to them. That's one massive data bank guiding you!

You could not possibly keep all that information that is shaping your decisions in your conscious mind. Imagine waking up and saying, "Now, let's see. Who am I?" After figuring that out, you then say, "And what must I do now? Oh, I know. Open my eyes. And what do I do next to get myself up? Oh, I remember. Toss back the covers. Then my right leg goes over the side of the bed and then my left. Okay, now step down. Then…"

That's what I meant about never making it out of bed. Efficient functioning, in fact functioning at all, requires that much of the internal information processing that shapes our everyday decision-making occur outside of our conscious awareness.

But aware of it or not, our internal physiological signals, thoughts, feelings, images, memories, and beliefs—all this chemical, electrical, physical, and mental stuff—continues feeding our sense of who we are and impacts how we solve problems, make decisions, and whether and what kinds of action we take.

If you are satisfied with how you are functioning and managing your life, all this non-conscious activity is fine. But if the ways you feel, think, and act are not serving you well, it is probably time for you to make some personal changes. Changing requires you get in touch with some of those internal influences that have been operating outside of your direct awareness and bring them to the surface, into consciousness, so you can work with them.

That makes sense, doesn't it? If your car started giving you trouble, you or your mechanic must first look under the hood, analyze, and test to determine what's causing the trouble. Only then are you in a position to decide how best to fix it.

Personal problems work that way too. Take-charge living means looking under your psychological hood, analyzing and testing, figuring out what you are doing that contributes to the cause of your troubles or unhappiness. You can't improve your life without knowing specifically what it is you are trying to fix.

Before continuing, I want to remind you of a very important point I made earlier. The change process focuses on you, not other people. As long as there is more than one way for you to respond to a situation, if you're not satisfied with the results you are getting with what you are doing now, that is what you work on changing. Ask yourself the following essential questions: Is what I am doing working for me? Am I moving toward, not away from, my goals? When the answer is no, then ask yourself: What do I need to change in my thinking or my behavior to turn things around?

Of course, some of your problems and frustrations may stem from things other people have done or unfortunate life events. However, the issue is still this: What are you doing about it? Are you handling the situations well or do you need to learn new strategies for living more effectively? Take-charge living does not involve spending your energy wishing, blaming, maneuvering, or demanding others change. Taking your show on the road and learning to live a take-charge life is about strengthening yourself so you can deal more effectively both with others and yourself.

## Getting In Touch With Your Inner Actor

Let's take stock of where we are. We've established that our bodily or physiologic reactions, thoughts, feelings, and behavior are intimately interconnected and influence each other continuously. Out of necessity, much of the work occurs outside of our conscious awareness. We have also established—if you want to change something about the way you think, feel, or act—you must first understand what is going on inside you so you know what exactly you're trying to fix. Most likely, some of what's going on that contributes to the problem is below the level of conscious awareness. I don't mean it's permanently buried or deeply repressed, even though some traumatic things are. I simply mean, as I said in the last section, that as a practical matter we can't keep most of the internal information that moves us along from moment to moment within conscious awareness. There's just too much information continually being processed for that. Consciously, we are aware of only a fraction of what we actually sense and perceive. Most cortical (that is, higher brain) level-sensory processing occurs outside our awareness.

Ongoing activities being expressed without our conscious awareness are sometimes referred to as implicit processes, in contrast to explicit conscious processes. Those implicit processes are fine for routine day-to-day functioning, but we need to bring some of that material to the surface so we can work with it when we want to make important changes in ourselves. That poses something of a challenge. As complex as people are, it is sometimes hard to see where to begin with so much happening inside. I'll use the example of Juliette, a fifty-one-year-old artist, to clarify how to proceed.

Juliette's mom, who died a couple years ago, had been aggressively successful in business, a go-getter with high energy and low tolerance for any display of negative feeling or disagreement. When Juliette was growing up, the mother was also an alcoholic. Her heavy drinking caused irrational emotional explosions. Juliette remembers cowering in the corner, thinking she was going to die while her drunk, raging mother lunged and beat her over the head and shoulders with a book. Mind you, Juliette had not even misbehaved.

Juliette learned the best way to survive in that household was to be a very good girl, walk on eggshells, never ask for anything, and never be a burden. She also learned to blur what was going on inside her—"fuzz her mind over" as she put it—to make the pain and anger bearable. "Fuzzing" her thinking became such a deeply engrained habit that, as an adult, Juliette's thoughts were disconnected from her feelings. Her speech was vague, and she had great difficulty articulating things clearly. She feared standing up for herself about anything, and was so sensitive to being hurt that any upsetting thing someone else did or said could send her into an emotional tailspin for days.

One of Juliette's take-charge living goals was to deal more assertively with her sister. Juliette felt her sister demeaned her by treating her like an incapable child. She also felt her sister was sometimes openly rude to her. In therapy, she had been practicing paying closer attention to which feelings went with which thoughts, bodily reactions, and mental images. To help her along, Juliette answered the questions in the following Survey of the Problem. Let's see what we can learn from it about changing ourselves on our own.

## Survey of the Problem

**What is the troublesome situation?** My sister talks to me in a condescending way. She treats me as if I am a child. She also acts as if things I can't help, like having to work and not being able to go somewhere with her, are my fault. She can be very nice and very funny, but she also knows how to stick the knife in. I either shut up or stay away from her because I don't think I can do anything about the way she treats me.

**How would you like to respond to the situation that is different from how you currently respond?** Be specific and focus on how you would like to respond, not how you would like others to respond.

I would like to tell her to not use that tone of voice with me. I would also like to tell her to not keep repeating things I cannot do anything about—like going on vacation with her.

When we go out with friends to dinner, I would also like to speak up more instead of sitting quietly and letting her do all the talking, the way I usually do. Most of all, I'd love to tell her to stop taking digs at me.

## Scenario One

Close your eyes. Imagine you successfully did these things just the way you would like to do them.

A. **What feelings, mood, emotions does that produce?** I feel happy. I also feel proud of myself. It makes me feel powerful.

B. **What bodily reactions do you have when you imagine being the way you would like to be?** I am not nervous around her anymore. My body is relaxed, solid, and calm. If you took my blood pressure, it would be low. My voice is firm. I'm smiling, too.

C. **What beliefs, ideas, thoughts do you have now that you are acting as you wish to act?** Mainly, I'm pleased with myself. I am thinking, now that I've done this, I can do it again. I imagine my sister will be shocked at the change in me. I like that. I am thinking it is a shame I waited so long to learn to do this.

D. **What images come to mind when you see yourself being successful at being assertive with your sister?** I thought of a cat named Teresa Tigertail I used to have. She was so smart and patient. Nothing scared her. She even attacked dogs. I also see myself being taller. Maybe I'm standing straighter. I don't know. Anyway, I feel taller. Lots taller. And smarter. Like my mind suddenly got sharper.

### Scenario Two

Close your eyes. Imagine planning to really try to speak assertively to your sister today.

A. **What feelings, mood, and emotions does that produce?** I feel scared. Nervous. I want to leave.

B. **What bodily reactions do you have now or do you think you'd have at the time, when you imagine speaking up today?** I get tense. I can feel my chest get tight, and my heart goes faster. Even right now, my jaw is clenched. I know I couldn't look her in the eye. Probably my voice would be almost a whisper. I don't think I could do it. Just thinking about it makes me nervous.

C. **What beliefs, ideas, thoughts do you have about speaking up to her?** For one thing, she is smarter than I am. She always wins an argument. She'd probably just laugh at me or ignore what I say. I don't know. Maybe she'd get mad. Maybe she wouldn't talk to me anymore.

D. **What images come to mind when you see yourself trying to be assertive with your sister?** Jumping off a cliff! Just thinking about it makes me feel like I'm five years old. I can't do it. I really can't. Besides, if I could—which—I can't—I'd be such a bitch.

Quite a contrast, isn't it? When Juliette imagines successfully dealing with her sister, she feels proud, happy, and powerful. She thinks positively about herself. Her body is relaxed, and she associates her assertive behavior with images of strength, intelligence, and growth. When she imagines actually taking the necessary steps (that is, really speaking openly to her sister about the things bothering her), she is frightened. Her body knots, and she imagines herself pained but helpless to do anything about the nasty treatment her sister dishes out. Juliette pictures herself so childlike that she is paralyzed. On top of that, she believes that asserting herself would make her a bitch. Bottom line, Juliette would just as soon jump off a cliff as stand up for herself.

What this tells us is that Juliette's resistance to change stems from a negative inner belief system (not all of it necessarily in her conscious awareness) about what changing her ways would mean. That belief system is a stew of negative images, thoughts, emotions, and bodily reactions about fear, helplessness, and paralysis while trying to assert herself with her sister. It also includes feelings about her body growing tense and her voice fading away, thinking she is dumb, and anticipating being ignored and maybe even permanently abandoned by her sister. With such a sinister system of ideas and feelings operating, little wonder the mere thought of exerting some control of her relationship with her sister strikes fear in Juliette's heart.

In the next chapter, we will take a closer look at these internal fear-inducing beliefs. They operate like switches being pulled in the basement of your mind without you even knowing it, which is okay if things are going well for you. But if you're playing the lead in your very own soap opera, those basement beliefs have too much control. We need to drag them into the spotlight, get a closer look at them, and, most importantly, do something about them.

# 4

## *Conquering Stage Fright*

✦

### *How to Overcome Your Fears of Changing*

An unwarranted, unrealistic, often unconscious fear of changing is the boogeyman that keeps people stuck. Why else would otherwise sensible people repeat the same losing patterns of behavior over and over again, even though logic and common sense tells them they should change?

Lucille is a bright, delightful woman of twenty-five. Currently a computer programmer, she loves acting and dreams of nothing but turning professional. She received rave notices while starring in several major college productions. Since then, she has received standing ovations for her work with an amateur theater group. Despite her successes, Lucille, unresponsive to encouragement from her acting coach, who is become quite frustrated with her, delivers one excuse after another for why she does not go out on auditions. When changing is not objectively dangerous—and it certainly isn't in Lucille's case—what keeps her from pursuing the work she so passionately loves?

To answer that question, I need to tell you something about internal barriers to change that people like Lucille unintentionally erect, keeping them mired in one unhappy circumstance or another. Internal barriers are a witches' brew of negatives reactions about our ability to change our behavior—a mix of negative ideas, negative images, negative beliefs, negative physical reactions and negative emotions.

Recall Juliette. Because she sees her sister as smarter and pushier, Juliette believes she could never hold her own conversationally and would look like a fool if she tried. The reality of Juliette's situation is that her sister is more verbally facile, but not smarter. Juliette has all the verbal skills she needs, she's just afraid to try them out. She lacks what psychologist Albert Bandura calls "perceived self-efficacy." That's another way of saying she lacks a belief in her ability to cope effectively with the situation. Remember, she does not really lack the skills to cope effectively. But as Dr. Bandura notes, unless people believe they can produce desired effects by their actions, they have little incentive to act.[1]

Perceived self-efficacy goes beyond how we assess our skill level. It's also about how we assess our ability to emotionally cope with a situation. Some people fear experiencing the negative thoughts, emotions and bodily reactions that are likely to get stirred up when they try altering their stuck behavior. When she imagined speaking up to her sister, Juliette feared feeling scared and feeling like she was being bitchy. Her chest would tighten. She would be unable to make eye contact with her sister and even lose her ability to speak.

Mind you, such thoughts and feelings, even though they are quite an unpleasant experience, are not realistic barometers of danger and do not necessarily mean we need to stop from moving ahead. But if we are so scared of what we have stuffed down inside, (our own thoughts and feelings), that we're not even in touch with them and don't know what they are, then blocking us from moving ahead is exactly what they will do. And we won't understand how come.

Lucille, the actress, avoided auditions because she began trembling every time she imagined being on stage with professionals. It took some rooting around in her mental basement but she finally figured out why. Her internal barrier to change, which she did not have any prior awareness of, was a nightmarish scene playing on the stage of her unconscious mind. The dialogue, with accompanying visuals, went something like this:

> *I'm an untalented fool. I have a lot of nerve to think I might act professionally. Growing up, I remember my mother always yelling, "You'll never amount to anything, you dumb kid!" I'm the kiss of death. I'd ruin everything if I had the audacity to find my way onto a professional stage. I can see it all. Opening night. A packed house. I walk on stage and screw up my cues and my lines. They try prompting me, but I keep screwing up. The audience boos. I single-handedly destroyed the entire production! The other actors, enraged, chase me down the aisle and out of the theater. Humiliated and shamed, I live in hiding in a dank, little basement apartment for rest of my life!*

I assure you that we could be the world's most fabulous actors, but we would not go on auditions either if we walked around believing that about ourselves.

---

1 Albert Bandura, "A Sociocognitive Analysis of Substance Abuse: An Agentic Perspective," *Psychological Science 10, no 3* (1999): 214.

Here is another example of basement barriers to change. Think of the millions of people who truly wish to stop abusing drugs, food, or alcohol because it is messing up their lives. These people sincerely want to change and know how much better off they would be if they did. So why don't they? Sometimes it's even a matter of life and death and they don't change. Something pretty powerful must be operating here. Even though they express the desire to change, consciously or unconsciously, many of these self-abusers are terrified of changing, because they don't believe they can stand the emotional and physical stress of experiencing the urge to use and not giving in to that urge. In Bandura's language, they lack perceived self-efficacy to cope with their own intense feelings. People suffering with this problem often feel, that when the urge hits, they will explode from the tension unless they surrender to their urges. Feeling—and thus believing—they cannot learn to tolerate and manage that tension (which is not true) means feeling and believing they cannot change.

The point I'm trying to drive home is that the biggest internal barrier to change is perceived self-efficacy—our lack of faith in our ability to do what is needed to gain the desired results. Lack of perceived self-efficacy leads us to arrive at one or more of these self-destructive conclusions:

- I do not know what to do to change.
- I know what to do to change, but I do not have enough skill to do it.
- I cannot do what it takes to develop the skill I need to change.
- I cannot tolerate the feelings that behaving differently would stir up in me.

Once we buy into these beliefs, there is only one—very erroneous—conclusion to come to. Because of our personal shortcomings and limitations, we are stuck with things as they are!

Another internal barrier to change, yet another way of keeping ourselves stuck, is not so much about our beliefs concerning personal shortcomings, even though they are often part of the picture. This barrier is based on our beliefs about how others will judge us and react to us if we change. In these scenarios, people predict and heartily believe the most catastrophic things will happen to their relationships if they risk acting differently. They are certain others cannot or will not put up with their changes. In other words, doing things differently means rejection and abandonment.

The keyword describing this thinking is catastrophic. The man who is afraid to assert himself with his boss does not simply fear being fired. No, it is much worse than that. He is positive he will not only lose this job, but nobody else will hire him again. Not ever! That means he will go broke. Then his family will leave him. Finally, he winds up on the streets, a bagman for life. It is a catastrophic picture.

Take Juliette, our ongoing example. She scared herself with a hugely overblown threat that, if she spoke up to her sister, Anna, about things she did not like, Anna might never speak to her again. Despite Anna's inconsiderate, sometimes rude behavior toward Juliette, she loves Juliette and depends heavily on her for company and emotional support. In reality, there is no way Anna would quit talking to Juliette. However, in Juliette's way of catastrophic thinking, there is not a shred of doubt about it.

Fear of rejection plays in the background of many people's minds. The catastrophic fantasy is that others are prepared to abandon them because of the slightest disagreement. These people go through life keeping their opinions to themselves while smiling, shuffling, placating everyone, and never asking or expecting to have their own needs met.

An overblown fear of sounding stupid is another internal barrier to change. Nobody wants to say something publicly and sound foolish, but most of us could live with it if we did. For the person who imagines catastrophes, sounding foolish, even once, means losing respect forever. "Forever" turns it into a catastrophe. A bit extreme, I'd say.

Another catastrophic fear that plagues people is an anxiety of losing control in public, going or looking crazy, or saying or doing wildly embarrassing things. To counter that frightful possibility, such individuals are chronically uptight and overly controlled. Their mental radar forever scans for signs that they might be about to lose it. Ironically, such people are actually among the least likely people to be socially embarrassing.

The list continues with irrational catastrophic beliefs that people lay on themselves, terrify themselves with, and use as reasons for not changing. Such unrealistic, often subconscious beliefs, however unlikely to really come true, cause us to engage in avoidance behaviors. Avoidance is what blocks us from changing.

To complicate matters, fear and avoidance responses can be triggered instantaneously without you consciously knowing why. Professor Joseph LeDoux,[2] in his groundbreaking research showed that fear can travel along

---

2 Joseph LeDoux, *The Emotional Brain: The Mysterious Underpinnings of Emotional Life* (New York: Simon & Schuster, 1996).

two very different neural pathways. One pathway is a more conscious, "reasoned" cortical pathway. Because those reactions take complex cortical processing, they also take more time to occur. However, a thought or event that triggers fear can also travel instantaneously and unconsciously along a different pathway to a brain structure called the amygdala, producing an instant fear reaction without you necessarily knowing why. The reason does not matter at that point. Gut-level fear will cause you to engage in avoidance behaviors. Avoidance behavior is terrific if you are in real danger, such as jumping aside if a car is coming at you or evacuating if the movie theater catches fire. However, people also avoid situations because of dangers they imagine, exaggerate, and turn into catastrophes. Instead of moving forward, that keeps them stuck in bad situations when reason tells them that changing would make a lot of sense and brighten their lives.

Unnecessary avoidance behaviors—however necessary they may feel to you—are the critical factor in keeping psychological distress alive. It is important to be clear about the difference between unnecessary and necessary avoidance behaviors. Obviously, avoiding something that would be considered objectively dangerous by anyone's standards is necessary avoidance. However, do not fool yourself into labeling what are really unnecessary avoidance behaviors as necessary. I hope you will hear me when I tell you that the important role unnecessary avoidance behaviors play in keeping your life stuck cannot be overestimated. Neither can teaching yourself the difference between necessary and unnecessary avoidance.

## Your Interpreting Brain, an Endless Scriptwriter

When I say avoidance behaviors, I mean any behaviors on your part—mental or physical—that keep you from acting in ways you wish to act, that is, ways you believe would be best for you to act. Avoidance behaviors can take any or all of these forms:

- Physical avoidance (sitting idly in front of the television when you should be writing a term paper)
- Verbal avoidance (saying yes when you want to say no)
- Thinking (cognitive) avoidance (repeatedly telling yourself things that keep you from pursuing your goals, such as "I'm stupid…I'm ugly…I'm a klutz…I'm inadequate…I'm *fill in the blank…*"; Another form cognitive avoidance is not resolving a problem because you don't let yourself think about it.)

- Emotional avoidance (avoiding change because it causes anxiety but not being in direct touch with that anxiety, so you do not know why you avoid it)

Avoidance behaviors accomplish two things. They help you avoid doing constructive things, and they help you avoid stopping yourself from doing destructive things. Either means we avoid trying out new thoughts and new ways of acting that would bring greater satisfaction to our lives. Obviously then, putting an end to your avoidance behavior is a major key to changing yourself.

How do you do that? To begin to answer that question I need to tell you about the brain's endless quest for meaning. When I first read this idea some years ago in an article by Dr. Michael Gazzaniga, a noted physiological psychologist, I was startled. However, the more I thought about it, the more obviously true it seemed. Based on extensive research about the brain, Dr. Gazzaniga said the human brain, as part of our basic survival mechanism, is hardwired to *interpret* the ceaseless flow of information it encounters.[3] If you stop to think of the vast quantities of information that flow nonstop from within our body to our brain as well as arrive at our brain via our five senses from the world around us, that is a staggering task.

By interpret, I mean, based on all its prior experiences, memories, learning, and stored images, as it receives new input, your brain must categorize and explain that input to itself. The brain must decide, "What does this input I'm receiving mean?" This does not mean your brain's explanation to itself is always accurate. It isn't. However, the explanation it produces, based on everything you have come to be until now, is what your brain adopts and believes.

It was not too long after, at a colloquium in 1990 at UCLA, that I heard psychologist Dr. John Bargh explain how his research has demonstrated the brain goes an important step further. Beyond simply deciding what the input means, the brain very quickly and efficiently (but not necessarily consciously) uses specialized neural circuitry to assess and evaluate the input, that is, to size it up. Basically your brain wants to know, "Is this information I'm receiving about some thing that is good for me so I can go toward it? Or is it bad for me, in which case, I should avoid it?" Whether you are aware of it or not, your decisions to act or not act in specific ways are based on these ongoing assessments.

---

3 Michael S. Gazzaniga,. "The Social Brain," *Psychology Today*, November (1986): 29.

We now come to a fascinating twist in the story. One key source of input to the brain is your own behavior, the things you actually do. Your brain watches you and pays close attention to how you behave. It then uses that behavior—correctly or incorrectly—as evidence of what it will believe.

If your brain sees you avoiding something, it concludes that what you are avoiding is somehow dangerous. By dangerous, I mean you risk some awful consequence if you did what you are avoiding doing. Otherwise, why would you avoid doing it? Of course, your beliefs and feelings that lead you to avoid something may not be accurate reflections of realistic danger. That is irrelevant. The brain trusts and believes what it sees you do. If you avoid doing something, it figures, "Hey, you know what you're doing. There's danger here." Therefore, it buys into that idea and signals you to continue avoiding. You now return the favor, believing the brain must be right because it is your brain and brains are for knowing things. So, you continue to avoid. Your continued avoidance simply reinforces the brain's belief that it is too risky for you to act any differently. You see where all this is going. Exactly nowhere. It is a closed circuit as your mind and body listen to a negative loop tape.

To bring this idea to life, I'll tell you about Jane, a woman suffering from extreme shyness. If we had a printout of the looping, negative inner dialogue between her brain and body, it might sound something like this:

Brain: Changing would be wonderful. You're way too shy. That's why you're so lonely.

Body: I know. I'd give anything to change. I've tried, but I simply can't.

Brain: I know you can't. Even when you just think about it, I see how you freeze up. Speaking up must be very risky and way too dangerous. If not, you wouldn't freeze up like that.

Body: Exactly. Even just thinking about trying gives me the shakes, and my jaw locks up.

Brain: Yes, those shakes and the locked jaw prove how risky it is. Don't push it. Awful things could happen.

Body: Exactly. I'm glad you agree! My gut instinct told me all along there's nothing I can do to fix this problem. It's ridiculous to try or even think about.

Brain: Yup!

When you think about it, this is pretty wild stuff. Jane's reasoning brain has read books. She knows full well there are various things people do to overcome shyness, such as go into therapy, join a support group like Toast

Masters, or read self-help books. She understands nobody ever overcame shyness by sitting home thinking about it. Jane gets it that bottom line, conquering shyness requires getting out of the house and starting to act differently, even if it's one baby step at a time, and without that nothing is going to change.

But logic collapses when Jane's brain watches Jane hide from social situations. Hiding—not reason and logic—counts. Her behavior, not her book knowledge, impresses her brain and determines what it will accept as truth and reality. It does not matter that Jane's fears and her hiding from people are based on her extremely inaccurate assessment of her ability to learn to do otherwise and what would happen if she tried. Over any other information it may have, her brain bases its beliefs on what it observes her doing. It buys into Jane's story that it is too risky to try overcoming her shyness. It not only buys into the story, but it actively encourages her to continue avoiding people, even though shyness leaves her lonely and aching for connection. The behavioral tail wags the logical dog.

What's so tragic is that Jane's beliefs about overcoming shyness are completely wrong. Despite how gut level true and accurate her beliefs and emotions feel to her, the reality is that Jane could do a lot to overcome her shyness, if she would only try.

Overcoming personal obstacles to change is exactly what the next part of this book is about. It gives you an approach and action steps to take in order to change any of your behavior that hinders you from living a more fulfilling life. To help you move forward with that, you will also learn how to manage the negative thoughts and feelings that have stopped you from changing in the past.

Not that all of us don't sometimes avoid doing unpleasant things. But when that avoidance is chronic, or seriously damages the quality of your life, it's a problem worth doing something about. If you're stuck doing the same old things that get you nowhere, and losing out on life because of it, it's time for you to learn ways to take better care of yourself.

## The Theater of the Emotions (The Script Ain't Necessarily So)

I've been talking about people believing things that are untrue about themselves and then using those beliefs as the basis for avoiding change, even if changing would make them a lot happier. How do people come to create such negative, life-limiting scripts about themselves? And once set in place, why do those scripts stick like glue, no matter what evidence the person may have to the contrary?

I want to give you a closer look at some of the forces that help shape our views of ourselves. When these forces have been mostly positive and life-enhancing, people enjoy wonderful benefits, such as self-confidence, productivity, good relationships, and inner contentment. If we are among the less lucky ones or if the major forces influencing us (especially during childhood and adolescence) promoted low self-esteem and a poor self-image, it is so much easier to feel stuck and settle for a second or third-rate life as adults.

I assume you are reading this book because your life feels a little (or maybe a lot) stuck. Do you need more independence? Are you pursuing your goals? Perhaps emotional happiness is missing. Whatever your needs, dreams, or goals, it helps to understand how and why you initially developed your self-limiting ideas if you yearn for change. A peek into the past helps ready you for directing a happier personal show.

We humans are enormously complex creatures. At any given moment, each of us is like an incredible, unique tapestry, an exquisite, intricate interweaving of all the threads of our past experiences with what is happening today. Ideas, images, symbolic representations, muscle memories, emotions, feelings, physical sensations, bodily movements, as well as verbal and nonverbal behaviors (that is, the countless personal life experiences each of us has stored in memory), in concert with our basic biology and physiology, influence how we feel, what we think, and what we are willing to do or not do. This learning and stored memories are powerful forces and very much a part of our survival system. Most of the time, it pays to listen to what they are telling us. Past learning guides us through the multitude of mundane things we do each day as well as help us maneuver through complex challenges, decision-making, and problem-solving, everything that makes up human living.

Trouble ensues if those past experiences have caused us to store beliefs that are not particularly accurate assessments about who we are, what we are capable of, or how things are in the world. Especially when such beliefs take root under heavily emotional circumstances, they remain emotionally loaded and feel compellingly true at a gut intuitive level. It is difficult not to follow a message about yourself when it comes from deep inside you, feels compelling, and you are positive it is true. Our resistance to doubting such beliefs, to questioning their veracity, is enormous. So, is the initial resistance we have to changing them. That makes sense, doesn't it? No matter how inaccurate, why would any of us just dump a strong belief about ourselves that we have held for years? We wouldn't. It takes coaxing, effort, and knowing the right steps to take and how to reward yourself for effort. That is the reason for this book.

Some of the most powerful emotional conditioning of beliefs about ourselves takes place in childhood. Picture for example, a child who is constantly criticized, called stupid, belittled and berated by the parents. Keep in mind that as a child:

- We are dependent. We need and want protection as a matter of survival because we cannot strike out on our own.

- Our knowledge of the world as well as our capacity to understand and reason is very limited.

- Our brain, by virtue of its hardwiring, seeks to explain to itself what is happening to us.

- We, like all children, have a tendency to see ourselves as the center of things.

The child in my example may be a perfectly lovely little boy or girl, not stupid or bad at all. However, the child does not know that. All the child knows is that it's the parents who are the authorities. What they say must be so, and what they say hurts, arouses fear, and causes self-recrimination. True to a child's way of thinking, this youngster, in its hunger for love, reasons, "It's my fault. If I were better, they would love me. They wouldn't say bad things about me." Obviously, strong, emotional feelings are attached to these ideas.

However, these ideas and feelings are occurring within the confines of an immature body and mind, so they are not subject to reasoned scrutiny. In fact, just the opposite is true. The child internalizes the criticisms, whole and undigested. They then remain, embedded in the emotional gut, into adulthood. Impervious to reason or contradiction, they block the passage of new ideas and create symptoms of depression, anxiety, rage, and low self-esteem.

As a result, this adult, who is really a very okay person, sets limited goals, gets into abusive relationships, or allows others to walk all over them because the person still believes and acts out the old script from childhood. "I'm inadequate...I'm bad...What goes wrong is my fault...If I try to do things right, I'll screw up...I'm a loser...I don't deserve better."

If you try to reassure a person like this that they shouldn't think that way, they're really terrific and they just don't appreciate themselves enough, what do you think happens? Chances are you have had the experience of trying to convince self-critical people to ease up on themselves, appreciate their qualities and stop thinking so negatively. Maybe people have tried convincing you of that. Either way, you know it doesn't work, especially if the bad feelings have been around since childhood.

Why doesn't common sense, even with solid evidence and demonstrated proof, prevail? Because the self-critical person not only believes the opposite, those beliefs are tightly tied to strong emotions. Intense emotions make the belief feel one hundred percent true. Forget that you can point to ten ways it isn't so. The self-demeaning person will "Yes, but" you every time:

> Yes, I hear what you're saying, but you don't really understand. I know myself better than you do. I'm not okay. I can't succeed. I'm unlovable. I'm *fill in the blank…*

In his seminal book *Feeling Good,* Dr. David Burns labels this form of distress-producing thinking as emotional reasoning. To quote from his book:

> You take your emotions as evidence for the truth. You logic: "I feel like a dud, therefore I am a dud." This kind of reasoning is misleading because your feelings reflect your thoughts and beliefs. If they are distorted—as is quite often the case—your emotions will have no validity. Examples of emotional reasoning include "I feel guilty. Therefore, I must have done something bad"; "I feel overwhelmed and hopeless. Therefore, my problems must be impossible to solve"; "I feel inadequate. Therefore, I must be a worthless person"; "I'm not in the mood to do anything. Therefore, I might as well just lie in bed"; or "I'm mad at you. This proves that you've been acting rotten and trying to take advantage of me."
>
> Emotional reasoning plays a role in nearly all your depressions. (I would add that emotional reasoning plays a role in nearly all other negative feelings as well. MJ) Because things feel so negative to you, you assume they truly are. It doesn't occur to you to challenge the validity of the perceptions that create your feelings.
>
> <u>One usual side effect of emotional reasoning is procrastination</u>. (Emphasis MJ's.)[4]

---

4 David D. Burns, *Feeling Good: The New Mood Therapy* (New York: New American Library, 1980, 37).

Emotional reasoning is our biggest roadblock to personal change, that is, our biggest obstacle to take-charge living. It is us telling ourselves, "If I feel something, it must be true. The stronger I feel it, the more it proves what I believe is true." The fact of the matter is that the intensity of our feelings is not proof of the truth of what we believe. The intensity of our feelings is nothing more than just that—intense feeling—no more, no less. Intense feelings may represent a true belief, or a belief that is totally inaccurate.

To hammer home the point, I will use a somewhat extreme example. Imagine a woman suffering from agoraphobia. She has such a terrifically strong fear of leaving home and being out in public that she never does it. What could possibly keep someone a prisoner in her own home year after year with all the attendant anguish such a lifestyle inflicts on the woman as well as her family? Emotional reasoning, that's what!

It all started when the woman—I'll call her Kate—was in a high-stress period. One fateful morning, her stress revved even higher by several cups of coffee, Kate was walking around a department store when suddenly, without warning, she was overcome with panic. Knowing nothing about panic attacks, Kate did not understand what was happening to her. Whatever it was, because of the intensity of the arousal she felt, it must be something calamitous. Her brain immediately swung into action, doing what human brains are hard wired to do—come up with an explanation. Not totally illogically, given how wild and out of control she felt, Kate's brain concluded she must be going crazy. What else could account for such an out-of-control, alien state of being?

Terrified, desperate, and shaking so hard that she could barely drive, Kate somehow made it home. But everything associated with that awful experience—being out in public, being in a large store, being far from her car, feeling inexplicably wild inside and certain she was going to start screaming and make an utter fool of herself in front of all those people until they finally came and hauled her away to the funny farm in a butterfly net—all this became firmly locked into Kate's memory. It powerfully shaped a new belief that she was at the ragged edge of insanity. Thus began Kate's process of paralyzing her life with a fear of going crazy. Keep in mind, medically speaking, none of what Kate believes about going crazy could possibly come true, regardless of how intensely she believes and feels it. Kate is not now—and cannot and will not become—psychotic. Nevertheless, she suffers dreadfully from the fear she might.

What really happened? Kate hyperventilated because of stress. Hyperventilation caused a decrease in her body's supply of oxygen and carbon dioxide. That oxygen and carbon dioxide shift in the balance of her blood chemistry (not impending insanity) caused the symptoms (the sweating, wooziness, dry mouth, and racing heart) that so scared Kate.

Nevertheless, Kate is hooked on her brain's assessment and interpretation of the episode, namely she was on the brink of going crazy. The fear of going crazy and her deep belief it could easily happen are now strongly wired to those intense feelings in the department store and her memories of how awful the experience was. Further, she concludes it could—and very likely will—happen again. So she begins the process of avoiding. And the more she avoids, the more her brain is convinced she's right to do so. Leaving home is dangerous. If it were not, she would do it.

Admittedly, Kate's situation is somewhat extreme, but not that uncommon. It certainly offers a striking example of how emotional reasoning works. "I have a strong feeling about what I believe, and that strong feeling proves my belief is correct."

What is the antidote to Kate's state of paralysis? It is the same for anyone whose life is stuck in some unwanted place. They must press themselves into at least the beginnings of some meaningful behavior change. (In Kate's case, that must be leaving the house. Initially, it would perhaps be only for short periods and not very far. Gradually, she would increase the time and distance.) A change in behavior away from the stuck place, in turn, will cause the brain to reassess its position that change is completely impossible because it is too dangerous. Little by little, the brain reevaluates the situation by watching the changed behavior. In turn, it quiets the emotions. That is why continuing to practice the new behavior becomes easier. Essentially, avoidance behavior must yield to nonavoidance. That is true for Kate, and it is equally true for you.

This chapter provided the first step to conquer the stage fright that prevents you from changing. To get your show on the road and keep it there (that is, to develop your unique talents to take charge of your life), you needed to understand how powerful internal forces generate emotional roadblocks that make the thought of changing feel so difficult, perhaps even impossible. I also talked about the importance of separating real threats and dangers from imagined or greatly exaggerated threats.

This understanding puts you way ahead of the average person's understanding of what is happening. However, understanding is only the first step. The essential issue is what to do about it. That is what the rest of the book is about. Step by step, you will practice learning how to create a more fulfilling role for yourself, go through rehearsals at home, handle irrational fears and emotional resistances to change, and finally try out and continue fine-tuning your new performance out in the real world.

# 5

# *Going Solo*

✦

## *How to Pinpoint Your Specific Goals*

### Where Is It Best To Start?

Think of a beautiful tree. We would never ask which is more important. The roots or the trunk? The branches or the leaves? It's understood that all the parts of the tree are essential to its creation and growth.

The same is true with people, except, instead of roots, trunks, and the like, our complex interactions are among our emotions, physiology (bodily reactions), thoughts, and behavior. Think of them as four systems, each in nonstop communication with the others, shaping who we are, how we feel, and what we are willing to do. When we decide to be an Eliza Doolittle, that is, to change something about ourselves in order to move our life forward, we will have to cause changes in all of these four systems. What is the best way to do that?

Bodily or physiologic reactions do not lend themselves to your direct manipulation. Say you have a big speech coming up and the thought of talking to so many people is creating knots in your stomach. You have no way of reaching into your gut and directly untying those knots.

Similarly, feelings, including moods and emotions, do not lend themselves to your direct manipulation. There is no feeling fuse box or switch for you to throw into the off position. You certainly experience feelings directly, that's for sure, but you cannot work directly on changing them. Say you feel fearful. We all know that simply telling the feeling to go away will not get rid of it. Even though you cannot erase negative feelings, there's a lot you can do to manage them in a way that minimizes their impact.

We start with a very important principle: Feelings are not facts. Quite often, the feelings keeping you from acting in your own best interests are actually lying to you. Despite what the feelings tell you, what feels true to you is likely to not be objectively true. Let that idea sink in because it is one of the most important things you can learn from Take-Charge Living. Just because you feel something doesn't make it true! Some of your strongest feelings, the very ones that make you resist change, are likely to be merely old, incorrect assumptions you have been carrying around for years. These assumptions have never been tested out and are not based on demonstrable fact. They are simply assumptions, not facts. Only you have been treating them as facts.

That's good news. What it means is, even though certain feelings are unpleasant for you to experience and they feel true to you, if they are not based on objective fact—that is, if there's no hard evidence to prove they are true—you can begin to learn you do not have to take them so seriously anymore. There is a big difference between tolerating an unpleasant feeling you know is just a feeling and not a fact and being controlled by the feeling because you believe it represents truth and reality. In the first instance, you can feel uncomfortable, but you will move forward and make changes anyway. In the second, you will feel too scared to act.

That was certainly the case for Isabella, a likeable, knowledgeable, very bright, devoted wife and mother, a successful fighter for political causes, but so overly intense. At the age of sixty, Isabella felt exhausted by her chronic need to assume way too much responsibility for the people and projects she cared about. Intense, wound up, and concerned, Isabella felt a physical knot in her stomach most of the time. Relaxing, even briefly, was next to impossible. The moment she began slowing down, her mind jumped to some task she felt must have her attention. Isabella's waking hours were a nonstop performance without any intermissions. She lived as if the world would stop functioning without her constant help. She sometimes even referred to herself as a "performing seal."

As smart, well read and psychologically sophisticated as she is, it came as a complete surprise to Isabella that her feelings—her urges to leap into action and the intense nervousness she felt until she did—were just old conditioned feelings, and it was not dangerous if she sometimes chose to ignore them, sit still, and let the world take care of itself. She was even more surprised to realize the urge to help, really to rescue, came from many painful childhood experiences where she was thrust between two warring parents who expected her to mediate their conflicts and soothe them.

Armed with this understanding, Isabella was determined to change. She knew she could not simply wish away that old script and all the associated feelings, but she sure could do things to cause a heavy rewrite. Following the six acts of Take-Charge Living, Isabella developed a successful program to retrain herself not to try rescuing everyone all the time. What helped her pull it off was something she found to be a mind-blowing insight. Namely, it was not dangerous for her to not act. Keep in mind, her guts were reflecting the old script and telling her she was bad and it was dangerous not to jump to action. That was the voice from her childhood. At the age of sixty, Isabella finally learned she had the freedom to not take the voice and the feelings it stirred up seriously anymore. The feelings did not go away immediately, although they did over time. But knowing her strong gut feeling was just a feeling and nothing more enabled her to feel safe in altering her behavior. That was the key to long-term, satisfying change.

Realizing your negative feelings are frequently inaccurate reflections of reality is an important first step in decreasing their hold over you. You can do even more to depower negative emotions by using a powerful technique called mindfulness, which I will teach you later. With mindfulness, it is as if you are behind a movie camera. You are looking at your own feelings as if they were outside objects you are observing and filming instead of something residing in your gut. That kind of distance and detachment between you and your bad feelings drains some of the oomph out of them. That helps you feel more in control of—instead of controlled by—your negative emotions.

But back to my original question of where to start the change process. Because feelings and bodily reactions are not the ports of entry to self-change, that leaves the other two other possibilities: our thinking (cognitive) system and our behavior (action tendency) system. As it turns out, each can work well as a target for your effort at assertive self-improvement. Targeting both thoughts and behavior gains the best results of all. Remember, all four systems—emotions, physiology, thoughts, and behavior—are in constant contact with one another and heavily impact each other. That is good news, too. By working directly on changing your unwanted thoughts and behaviors, you also indirectly cause changes in your bodily reactions and your emotions. Take-charge living teaches you how to do that constructively on a self-help basis, producing self-change by ridding yourself of unwanted thoughts and behavior patterns. By focusing your change efforts on two of these interconnected systems (thoughts and behaviors rather than feelings and bodily reactions), you create payoffs in all four.

My job is arming you with an understanding of exactly what to do. However, you will be operating like Eliza Doolittle and Professor Higgins rolled into one, that is, a person who transforms yourself. Basic to getting the job done is committing to putting serious effort—which means lots of practice—into the program spelled out in this book. I promise you it's worth it because it lets you climb into the driver's seat when it comes to how you live your life.

## Getting Down To Specifics—Changing What?

- **One Change at a Time.** Taking charge and making personal changes works best if you don't overwhelm yourself. So the first ground rule is: Work on one change at time. After one is in place, you move on to the next. Trying to work on more than one thing at a time is a recipe for confusion, discouragement, even throwing in the towel on the whole effort. Follow common sense instead. Pick one target to kick off your Take-Charge Living effort.

- **Surveying the Choices.** The next thing you must decide is which target. I want you to get very specific. Start by reviewing Checklist 1: My Relationship Roles, which you completed earlier. The checklist asked you to rate yourself in the six areas of independence, understanding, expressing your views, expressing emotion, positive attitude, and ability to cope. For any area in which you experience difficulty, you also indicated the type of relationship or the specific person you have the difficulty with. If you did not complete the survey earlier, take some time to do it now. Review your areas of difficulty and pick the one that feels most important to you to change. For example, let's say your chief concern and the behavior you want to change is in the Communicating with Others category. More specifically, your concern is communication with family. In that case, write "Communication with family" on the following line. Write your chosen problem area on the following line:

______________________________________________________________

- **Selecting the Target.** We are homing in on things, but you now need to become very specific. If communication with family was your chosen problem area, we need to identify exactly which family members you want to communicate with differently. Is the problem with everyone or only certain family members? Which ones? Name them. Is the communication problem with just with one specific person? Who? Write who you want to act differently with on the following line:

______________________________________________________________

Assuming you identified the individual or group of individuals you want to act differently toward, we can move to the next step. That involves becoming specific about the type of behavior you wish to change. Return to my communication with family example. Is it because you have trouble expressing all your views? Or is it only the ones directly critical of the other person, political opinions, or views that disagree with that family member's point of view? Do you have the opposite problem? Perhaps family members complain you act as if you have all the answers and do not listen to them. What do you do that makes them feel that way? In other words, what do you think you would benefit from changing? Recall my example about Juliette. When asked how she would like to respond toward her sister that was different from how she currently reacts, she specified four things:

1. I would like to tell her to not use that tone of voice with me.

2. I would also like to tell her to not keep repeatedly complaining about things I cannot do anything about, like not being able to get off work to go on vacation with her.

3. When we go out with friends to dinner, I would also like to speak up more instead of sitting quietly the way I usually do and letting her do all the talking.

4. Most of all, I'd love to tell her to stop taking digs at me.

These four issues relate to one another, but they are not exactly the same. I would ask Juliette to order them. Which would she want to work on first, second, third, and fourth? Perhaps she would pick the one causing her the most pain. Or perhaps she would pick the one that is least scary. The choice is hers. You too will need to state specific goals for changing your behavior. List your goals for changing your behavior toward your target person(s):

________________________________________________

________________________________________________

________________________________________________

________________________________________________

If you listed more than one goal, select and circle the goal you want to work toward first. We will use that as your target for practice throughout the rest of the book.

- **Six Keys to Unlocking the Change Process**. Pay close attention to these six keys. They tell you what it will feel like during the process of making an important personal change in yourself, that is, what to expect to happen. Oddly, most self-help books barely even discuss them. However, without a proper understanding of how people change, it is easy to become discouraged or think there is a problem when you are really progressing just fine. For example, many people think, once they have insight into their problem and know what steps they are supposed to take, they should be able to do it smoothly and make change happen quickly. People are not designed to change quickly. Unless they understand that up front, it is easy to feel discouraged and decide this take-charge living business may work for some, but it is not in the cards for them. They believe something about their personality, or maybe even something genetic, makes it impossible for them to change. So they throw in the towel on changing, erroneously concluding they are stuck with being as they are. It's really too bad if someone becomes unnecessarily discouraged because of wrong expectations about how change works. I want to prevent that from happening to you. A good grasp of the following six keys to unlocking the change process will start you on the right foot, giving you an accurate picture of what to expect as you work at self-transformation.

- **Key One:**

What Is Learned Can Be Unlearned and Something Better Put in Its Place. Perhaps you never thought of yourself as having learned the unwanted behavior you now want to get rid of, but that is what happened. Somewhere, you learned a certain way of thinking or doing something. You continued doing things that way so often that it came to feel like a natural part of who you are. Many of these thinking and behavior patterns we acquire in childhood by watching those around us, long before we understand what they mean. Some we learn in our adult lives as well. Habits—and that's what these learned patterns of thinking and behavior are—habits—can become ingrained in us so subtly or gradually that we may not even be aware it is happening. Once rooted, habits have a way of feeling like a basic part of our being. That is why, when we think about ridding ourselves of such habits, it can feel like an impossible mission. Fortunately, this is only a feeling, not a fact. Note, I said your habit was learned. That means your unwanted ways of behaving and relating to others aren't emanating from your genes. Nor are they some unchangeable part of your personality. Annoying though they may be, what you're trying to get rid of are only learned habits. If you think about it, that is great news. What is learned can be unlearned. Along with that, a new, more rewarding habit can be learned and put in its place. Let me give you an example from the physical instead of the psychological world. Say you just moved to England and need a car to get around. You're nervous about driving. The Brits drive on the opposite side of the road from us and their driver's seat is where our passenger seat is. You swallow hard, but you pay your money. Before you know it traffic is speeding by and you are struggling to drive on what your nervous system is conditioned to think is the wrong side of the road. That would be stressful enough, but forcing yourself into the middle of the intersection to make a right instead of a left turn is positively terrifying. What a horrible realization! Your ingrained, American driving habits are not doing you any good, and they might get you killed.

As a matter of sheer survival, you are very self-conscious and hyper-vigilant while driving. Your eyes stay glued to the road as you coach yourself, talking through each step of the way. However, driving British style becomes more familiar over time. After a while, it even begins feeling fairly natural. What you've done is force yourself to unlearn old driving habits and step-by-step build new habits. You naturally felt tense and vigilant initially, but as the new habits grew stronger with practice, you began relaxing and not having to think about it so much. Eventually, you could drive and chat with a friend, listen to the radio, or plan your day, the same as you did at home. Changing psychologically driven habits requires undergoing much the same process as changing physical habits like driving a car or altering your tennis game. There is nothing magical about either one. Both require time, a precise picture of what you are trying to accomplish, planning, repeated exposure, and systematically coaching yourself step by step in the new, more desirable ways of responding. Both feel odd, unnatural, awkward, and sometimes even scary at first. Essentially, psychological learning and change, which is what this book is all about, is much like physically learning to make a change in how you play a sport or dance. All of it takes time, practice, and willingness, at least initially, to endure some uncomfortable feelings. Learning new psychological habits to replace old undesirable ones is what my UCLA colleague and dear friend, Professor Gerald Goodman, would call a "boulders and BBs" problem. The old habit, with its familiarity and attached strong feelings, is like the boulder. It is big, solid, seemingly impenetrable, and impossible to move. The new habit you are trying to put in its place is like a BB. It is small, packs no punch, and is easy to ignore, push around, or toss out. If you continue working at personal change, guess what? Little by little, the BB chips away at the boulder. It saps the boulder of its strength and drains it of its power. At the same time, the BB grows bigger and stronger. Given sufficient time and practice, the BB becomes the boulder. The boulder then shrinks into a pea-sized object of little or no importance.

- **Key Two:**

You Need a Plan before You Try Changing Yourself. Would you build a house without blueprints? Would you walk on stage to act but ignore the script? Would you walk into a chemistry lab and spontaneously pour some of this and some of that into a beaker? Of course not. You recognize that each of these activities requires careful planning. Similarly, you must have a plan, a blueprint, or a road map, that is, something to guide you through the specifics of changing yourself. In the next section, I will show you exactly how to construct your personal change plan. Right now, I want to acquaint you with what to expect. I hope you have reviewed Checklist 1: My Relationship Roles and selected a target behavior. If not, this is the first step you need to take. Successfully changing yourself requires you specify exactly what it is you want to change.

After that, I will ask you to complete some mental imagery work. Imagination is a powerful tool. Using it to fullest advantage allows you to carefully prepare for change before trying to do it in real life. Going systematically through the change process via mental imagery lets you figure out ahead of time what actions you need to take at each step along the way. Mental imagery also helps you anticipate obstacles you may encounter, so you can plan for how to deal with them. This mental imagery work is an important aspect of making personal changes. Think how many rehearsals actors and the director go through to spot bugs and smooth out their performances. Well, you are both the chief actor and director of this play about how you want to act in life, which means lots of careful rehearsals. I will explain more about how to do this in the "Dress Rehearsals" section. The third piece of making your change plan focuses on your thinking. I assume thinking has gotten in the way of you changing in the past. Otherwise, you would have made the changes on your own and would not need this book. The task at hand is learning new ways to think about the changes you are undertaking, ways that are more conducive to promoting change than your old thinking patterns have been. The human mind, being what it is, we can safely anticipate that old patterns of negative thinking and feeling will crop up. Instead of you getting all wrapped up in worries, excuses, or irritations—the very thoughts that have kept you from moving forward in the past—we will talk about how to refocus your attention and energies onto the kind of thinking that supports your goals for change. To sum up, the three steps you will be using to make a plan for personal change are:

- Picking a specific target for change
- Using mental imagery to prepare for change
- Refocusing your thinking to support change

- **Key Three:**

Managing Resistance to Change. Negative feelings are inevitable when you begin breaking away from your old behavior patterns. Those feelings, along with your old ways of acting, are your boulders. The new feelings and behaviors you are trying to put in their place are the BBs. Of course, boulder-sized feelings will exert a powerful pull, urging you not to change. Worse, there is no way to quickly erase those negative feelings. That's a process that takes time. If you cannot immediately remove the negative feelings, the next best thing is to learn how to live with them, manage them, and not take them so seriously. That is really the secret. Let yourself experience a negative feeling without taking it so seriously. I will tell you more about that in the "Dress Rehearsals" section.

- **Key Four:**

Practice! Practice! More Practice! Change comes in steps that move you forward toward your targeted change. That means you step-by-step taking new actions, instead of repeating your old ways. You do not have to take giant steps, just steps. You do not have to feel like acting differently. Most certainly, when trying something new, you do not have to perform perfectly or even very well. Nevertheless, you must try new behavior. You must act. After giving it a shot, the next thing you do is take stock of how your new behavior went. What part went okay? Keep that. What would you change the next time? Include that in your planning and mental imagery work. Rehearse it in your head and in front of a mirror. Try it again in the real world. And so it goes. You practice and give yourself feedback. You fine-tune and rehearse your game plan. Then you practice more. There is no magic bullet for getting you from here to there. It is a matter of persistence and practice. I have faith you can do that. Surely you've stuck to some effort in the past even though you might not have felt like it. If you have done it before, you can do it again. Moreover, look at the reward—a life where you take control instead of letting life control you.

- **Key Five:**

Monitoring Progress. As you learn the steps and practice changing your behavior in the direction of take-charge living, it is a good idea to keep track of your progress. Keeping a simple record of what you have tried and your results does several things. If you are moving ahead, especially if the pace is slower than you would like, the written log is your proof you are indeed making progress. Should your efforts stall out, the written record lets you know that as well. That becomes your signal to review and revise your game plan, which is what any good coach would do.

- **Key Six:**

Self-Reward. One of my favorite topics is rewarding yourself. Recognizing and putting value on you, the good things you stand for, your qualities and positive abilities, is so essential to healthy living. In terms of following the action plan of Take-Charge Living, it is essentially required that you learn when and how to reward yourself. Sadly, too many people, especially those feeling distressed or dissatisfied with themselves, are only too eager to run a laundry list of their shortcomings. But ask them about their strengths—the things they do well or the things they like about themselves—and they come to a stop. To complicate matters, some folks believe self-praise is tasteless, boastful, and arrogant. Fortunately, if prodded a little, most people can find at least a couple of their assets. For one client of mine who grew up in a climate of nonstop criticism and pressure from his mother to perform to perfection, self-reward was simply a totally foreign idea. Not just foreign for himself, he honestly never realized that anybody else ever patted themselves on the back. I assured him they did. He trusted me not to lie to him, but smart as he was, he still could not figure out what value self-praise might have. He was truly amazed as he began learning how correctly assessing your own strengths and appreciating them is an important part of self-confidence and functioning effectively in this world. Also short on self-reward are those people who constantly look to others for approval and a reading on how they are doing. Positive self-assessment has no value to them because they distrust their own opinions. Only the stamp of approval from others gives them a way of approving of themselves. I regard appropriate self-reward that is based on realistic self-assessment as a keystone of success with the program outlined in this book. If you are going to take charge of your life, you must be the judge of yourself. Relying solely on the judgments of others to make you feel good or saying what is okay or not okay about you is giving away your power. Take-charge living is about empowering yourself. I don't mean you shouldn't care what others say or think about you. Feedback from others can be valuable to your personal growth and development. But the final judgment of who you are and how you want to be in this world rests with you. My friend Dr. Manuel Smith wrote a best-selling book about assertiveness, *When I Say No I Feel Guilty*. He lists being your own judge as a basic assertive right. He writes:

"You have the right to judge your own behavior, thoughts and emotions and to take the responsibility for their initiation and consequences upon yourself."[1]

---

1 Manuel J. Smith, *When I Say No I Feel Guilty* (Toronto: Bantam Books, (1975), 28.

# PART II
# Dress Rehearsals

*Practicing the Transformation*

# 6

# *Previewing a New Role (Act One)*

## *How to Use Mental Imagery to Create Your New Look and Sound*

This is where we go into action. I will become your action advisor, and you will become the action doer. If you have gotten this far, I assume you are at least seriously considering action to make some type of transformation in your life. "Your Action Guide in Six Acts" provides a step-by-step sequence of exactly what I will be asking you to do. Just to get a feel for where we are headed, please preview it. We will then get going. From there to the end of this book, it's all about doing. Only through taking action can you learn how to make the take-charge living approach work for you.

### Your Action Guide in Six Acts

- **Act One: Sharpening the Image of the Target Behavior**
  Chapter 6: Previewing a New Role: *How to Use Mental Imagery to Create Your New Look and Sound*

- **Act Two: Identifying the Enemies to Change**
  Chapter 7: Getting the Script Right: *How to Identify Your Enemies to Change*

  - Applying the Vertical Arrow Technique

- **Act Three: Your Plan of Attack**
  Chapter 8: Stepping On Stage: *How to Retrain Your Thinking and Plan Your Practice*

  - Creating Your Process Plan

- Take-Charge Thinking: The Stepping-Stone To Action
- Remaking That Movie in Your Mind
- Seven Scenarios For Tackling Thinking Errors
- Dumping Dysfunctional Thinking Patterns
- Applying the Active Dispute Technique

- **Act Four: Managing Your Feelings When They Resist Change**
  Chapter 9: Hitting the Right Emotional Note: *How to Manage Your Feelings When They Resist Change*

- **Act Five: Staging a Dress Rehearsal**
  Chapter 10: How Do You Get To Carnegie Hall?: *How to Stage Your Dress Rehearsals at Home*

  - Rehearsing Your Target Behavior at Home, a Step-By-Step Checklist

- **Act Six: Real World Trial Runs—Practice, Practice, and More Practice**
  Chapter 11: Taking Your Show on the Road: *How to Fine-Tune Your Performance*

  - Maintaining Accurate Expectations
  - Managing Emotional and Physical Arousal
  - Converting Threats to Challenges
  - Going From Easy to Hard in Small Steps
  - Repetition
  - Hooking Goals to Higher Order Values
  - Maintaining a Take-Charge Perspective

Earlier, I asked you to select a target behavior, one that represents an important change for you and a significant improvement over whatever you currently do. If you've got your target behavior, we are ready to move forward. But first, let's make absolutely sure you've picked a workable behavior change. Check it out against the following questions:

1. Is the behavior you wish to change your own behavior, not someone else's? Speaking up at staff meetings is an appropriate target behavior. Wanting your boss to call on you to speak more often is not an appropriate target. The first one is your behavior and within your control to change. The second is not.

2. Is the target behavior specific, observable, and not vague or general? If you told me what the target is, and I filmed you in action, could I tell with certainty by looking at the film, whether or not you are doing it? For example, you want to discuss differences you and your mate have about finances. Until now, you have gone along with your mate's way, even though you hate it. Maybe you have trouble asserting yourself or you are afraid your partner will not care for you as much, or whatever. Bottom line, your needs have not been made known. Now your goal is to make clear that you are not willing to continue to support overspending the family budget. If you say, "Honey, I think we are allowing ourselves to spend money we can't afford. We use the credit card as if we don't have to pay the bill at the end of the month. As a result, we are thousands of dollars in debt. That makes me very uncomfortable and anxious. I propose we make an agreement to immediately begin limiting credit card use to specific amounts a month. What do you think of that idea?" it would be clear to me that you are indeed engaging in specific, focused behaviors that directly address your target goal. In contrast, let's say you said to your mate, "Honey, I love the new table we bought for the living room, but do you think we maybe spent more than we should?" That's vague, passive, and indirect. "Honey" may guess you really have a larger issue. Then again, "Honey" may not. Even if "Honey" does, he or she may not help by saying so because, after all, "Honey" is the one who likes things the way they are.

Assuming you have picked a target for change and have it clearly spelled out on paper, we are ready to move on to shaping your image of yourself engaging in the new behavior.

## Firing Up Your Imagination

- Let's put your imagination to work. First, because it is so important, take a moment to double-check the target behavior you selected. Does it focus on your own behavior?

- Is specific and observable?

The next thing you need is a clear, detailed mental picture of exactly what you would look like when you are performing your new behavior. Having that picture of yourself locked into your mind is a road map to keep you from becoming confused, sidetracked, or even lost.

Two things are essential for a good mental picture. One, obviously, is your words. What specifically do you want to say? The other, equally important component is how you want to deliver your message. Besides saying the right words, what does your manner, body language, facial expressions, and tempo and inflections in your voice (that is, your other behaviors in addition to your words) need to look like to support your verbal message?

We'll start with your words. In a moment, I will ask you to close your eyes and think carefully about how you would like to state whatever it is you wish to say. First, to give you a feel for this, I'll use Juliette as my example again. When asked how she would like to respond to her sister that was different from her current way of reacting, she said, "I would like to tell her to not use that sharp tone of voice with me. I would also like to tell her to not repeatedly pester me about things I can't do anything about, like go on vacation with her."

As a goal, that is specific. However, Juliette can use many different ways to say things and meet that goal. Does she also want to express anger, be empathic, or sound emotionally neutral? The choice is up to Juliette. What you want to say and the emotional tone of it is a choice you need to make.

Whatever specific message you choose, some overall guidelines can help shape the verbal portion of your message:

- Decide ahead of time exactly what it is you want to say, including what emotional tone you wish to convey.

- Think of how to say your message concisely and to the point.

- Think of how to say your message with firmness and confidence.

- Think of how to say your message so it does not contains any long-winded explanations, excuses, disclaimers, put-downs, sarcasm, or inappropriate apologies.

- Choose words and tone of voice that remain respectful of the other person.

In Juliette's case, she decided she did not want to come across as angry—just firm—in letting her sister Anna know she wanted a change in how the sister speaks to her. Juliette also knew, given her history of letting Anna push her around and her fear of confronting her, she would be tempted to apologize profusely for even daring to question Anna. Part of Juliette's specific verbal goal was to avoid apologizing for speaking up.

Following Juliette's pattern, I would like you to decide what you want to say in your target situation. Be specific, be clear, be concise. What is the emotional tone you desire? Write it down. As you become more accustomed to this planning procedure, you may not need to write the message. Just thinking it through will be enough. At this stage of practice, writing it will help you sharpen your intended message.

Being effective takes more than words. Body language has a big impact on how we come across and whether others take our message and us seriously. I'll use Gwen, who suffers from excessive shyness, to illustrate what I mean. Gwen wants to ask her boss for a raise, which she certainly deserves. After months of putting it off, Gwen finally taps ever so lightly on the boss's door.

"Yes," says her boss, Lydia, barely looking up from her work. Gwen stands in the doorway with her head lowered while she rubs her hands together. "Well, what is it, Gwen?"

Gwen tugs at her earring and gives a little cough. "I…er…I…um…sure hope I'm not interrupting anything, Lydia. Heh, heh."

"It's okay. Sit down."

Seated, Gwen's body is tilted back, away from Lydia. She crosses her legs, uncrosses them, and recrosses them. Her face looks pinched. When she speaks, it is nearly a whisper. She hardly looks at Lydia. She mostly trains her eyes on the floor. Finally, after some irrelevant talk about one of the company accounts, Gwen spits out why she is there and asks for a raise. Gwen says the right words, but her meek voice and hesitant movements telegraph how nervous she is about doing this. Reading that, Lydia knows, if she chooses, she can easily turn Gwen down. Gwen will then leave without protest and maybe even apologize for taking up Lydia's time.

When you set about transforming something in how you act, in addition to what you say, all your other behaviors (body language, gestures, facial expressions, and inflection and tone of voice) must essentially support, highlight, and enhance your spoken message. To help you imagine yourself doing a good job of delivering your messages, here are some important pointers:

- Make eye contact.
- Keep your posture relaxed.
- Avoid nervous laughter or nervous joking.
- Avoid excessive or unrelated head, hand, and body movements.
- Avoid excessive pauses.
- Avoid hesitancy or stammering.
- Have facial expressions that are appropriate to what you are saying. For example, do not smile when you are saying something serious.
- Have appropriate loudness, tone, and inflection in your voice.
- Avoid whining, pleading, or sarcasm.
- Make sure your voice, posture, and body language are consistent with the message you want to deliver.

Occasionally people choose a target behavior that does not involve a conversation with others. Instead, it focuses exclusively on personal behavior that nobody else gets to see and internal conversations they have with themselves. Even so, the general outline of the "Your Action Guide in Six Acts" can be applied. I will give a brief example to illustrate.

I know a man named Lew, who is like Kate from an earlier example. He periodically suffers from panic attacks as well as a fear of going crazy. Unlike Kate, Lew is not housebound, quite the opposite in fact. He's highly social and professionally active in a rather high-risk law enforcement job. But at night, when he is alone at home, Lew spends endless hours reviewing in excruciating detail the many hurts and injustices he endured throughout his childhood, some thirty years before. At the same time, Lew's mental radar endlessly scans for signs of impending panic because he irrationally harbors the idea he might go over the edge with the panic and turn crazy one day.

Lew did have a very unfortunate childhood fraught with realistic fears of abandonment. As an act of survival, he learned to stuff down his true feelings while twisting his words and behavior to conform to the demands of his angry, often irrational mother. What Lew now experiences as a fear of going crazy is really a learned fear of getting in touch with his true feelings, many of them imprisoned since boyhood.

Lew's target behavior is to interfere with all this fearsome, negative ruminating and force his mind to think of things that connect to positive life experiences, for example, planning a ski vacation, starting his own computer consulting firm, and finding the right woman to marry and have a happy life with. Obviously, such a dramatic negative-to-positive thinking switch is a challenge, but Lew actually has taught himself to occasionally do it. However, he keeps tripping himself up with a catastrophic (completely illogical and purely superstitious) idea that, if he allows himself to be happier and think positive, planning, productive thoughts, he will be punished by going crazy. What a field day the psychoanalysts could have with that one! But our concern here is change. Improving Lew's life. Starting to get a new show on the road.

As you can see, going into action for Lew doesn't involve dealings with anyone else. This first step, which I call "Firing Up Your Imagination," in Lew's case, is about the script he must write for talking to himself. Using that script, once he begins implementing it, he will pull himself away from his ruminations, even in the face of powerful gut feelings telling him it is not safe to do so and threatening he will be punished for it. I am happy to report, by using the approach you will be learning in the coming chapters, Lew is already well on his way to transforming his thinking.

# 7

## *Getting the Script Right (Act Two)*

### *How to Identify Your Enemies to Change*

Is your motivation to change so high that you are prepared to go full-steam ahead, regardless of any interfering feelings or thoughts you may experience? If so, you are indeed fortunate. Most people contemplating a major personal change find the negative thoughts and feelings plus occasional negative physical sensations and bodily symptoms that get stirred up at the prospect of trying to change as their biggest barrier to getting going. It helps to get a grip on what all that negativity is about. I will tell you that it essentially always turns some perceived catastrophic threat to their self-esteem, safety, or well-being. Think about Lew's fear of going crazy. The threat, or at least its underlying meaning, has often been operating unconsciously, outside of the person's awareness. Lew for example, took his fear of going crazy at face value as a serious danger. He was clueless as to what that irrational fear was really all about.

Note, I said perceived catastrophic threat. When that threat, along with all its underlying meaning, is brought out into the open and made explicit, closer inspection almost always makes it clear (at least to the person's logical mind) that the chance of it really happening as imagined are highly unlikely, in fact close to impossible.

I will later teach you a very useful technique for flushing out these troublesome threats that may be operating underground in you, influencing your feelings, and hindering your change in behavior.

Before I say anything more about you changing yourself, let's make sure you have realistic expectations of how the change process works. The first thing I must tell you, even though I wish it was not so, is awareness and logic alone will not wipe out negative, resistant feelings that are likely to get stirred up within you when you think of really going ahead with some behavior change you have avoided until now. However, becoming aware of your underground messages and learning to think logically about them will help you cope with those negative emotions and resistance. Remember, all you need to do is tolerate those unpleasant negative and resistant feelings. You do not have to make them go away in order to take action.

Let's take a look at why gaining insight into those subterranean thought processes, while not a cure-all, definitely helps you tolerate and manage your negative feelings. That allows you, like Eliza Doolittle, to move into a role of self-transformation.

Exposing thoughts that have been operating outside of your conscious awareness until now lets you see more clearly the absurdity of some of these ideas that have been governing your life. That gives you a chance to refute them logically by presenting yourself with information you already know (that is, evidence you have in your possession) that shows them to be untrue. While awareness and logic won't make the bad feelings disappear, they will have some positive impact on how you feel. What I am saying is, even though you can't rid yourself of those negative vibes right away, you can do something to lessen their impact.

Another important part of assuming a proactive Eliza Doolittle stance is understanding these kinds of negative feelings that prevented you from doing things you want to do. However strong, unpleasant, and troublesome they feel, they are only feelings. Feelings are not facts. Nor are they signs of unmanageable threat or catastrophic danger to your well-being. Feelings are just feelings!

As you become accustomed to separating feelings of threat from being threatened in fact, a nice thing starts happening. You quit avoiding change and increasingly practice your new behaviors. A fascinating thing grows out of this. Your brain takes note that you are acting differently. It not only takes note, but it communicates this information to your emotional and information processing systems. (This intersystem communication happens via chemical and electrical reactions along very complex neural pathways that scientists are just beginning to map.)

Little by little, as you continue repeating this process—i.e., as you learn to tolerate your own negative feelings of resistance to change and do not take them seriously as real threats to you and you begin to practice your new, more desired way of acting despite the negative feelings—the negative feelings actually start fading away. After a while, as your negative emotional system calms down, you may even find practicing your new behaviors is fun.

Finally, just understanding your own feeling-reason connections empowers you. It's not that understanding gives you the power to make your negative or resistant feelings disappear, but a willingness to experience those negative feelings, because your new understanding makes them more tolerable, means you no longer avoid doing what you need to do. That is the start of the process of getting rid of those feelings. That act, of assuming some control over the situation—rather than feeling victimized and helpless to do anything about your feelings—in and of itself makes you feel better.

I hope I have convinced you how important it is for you to get in touch with the thoughts, which often operate below your level conscious awareness, that get in the way of you making constructive changes. Maybe you're thinking, "That's all well and good, but how do I make myself aware of something that is outside of my awareness?" For that, we turn to a wonderful exercise developed by the noted psychiatrist, Dr. David Burns, described in *Feeling Good,*[1] one of the most valuable self-help books available. Dr. Burns calls it the vertical arrow technique. I have adapted it to fit our self-transformation program.

## Applying the Vertical Arrow Technique

This exercise is best done on paper. Briefly, here is how the vertical arrow exercise works. You write down the negative thought, feeling or idea that gets in the way of you performing your target behavior. Then you ask yourself either one of these two questions, depending upon which question seems to fit best:

- If this idea is true, what would that mean to me?
- If this idea is true, what about it upsets me?

You make a little downward arrow to show the question was asked, and then you write a sentence (keeping it brief and pointed) that gives your answer to the question. The answer does not have to be logical or make a lot of sense. It just must be a candid statement of what you personally think or feel.

Next, you ask one of those same two questions about the answer you just wrote down. Then you make a little arrow, write the answer to that, and repeat the process over and over. Even when it sounds silly to ask, you keep going, pressing further and further down into your thinking until you come to a really catastrophic answer. Stop at that point. A couple of examples will make the sequence and reason for it clearer. I will start with Sue.

Sue, an exceptionally attractive, accomplished woman in her early thirties, is overly sensitive in the extreme to other people's reactions to her. She is quick to take offense and feel deeply hurt. When Sue has one of these

---

1 David D.Burns, *Feeling Good: The New Mood Therapy* (New York: New American Library, 1980, 235)

rushes of hurt and anger, she doesn't think clearly to consider alternative, less devastating explanations about what the other person's behavior might mean or how to react. The distress caused by one of these incidents can send her into an incapacitating emotional tailspin for hours, sometimes even days.

Sue's target behavior was preventing herself from automatically jumping to the worst possible conclusions. She wished to think more rationally and weigh alternative possibilities about the meaning of the other person's behavior. First, she needed to get a grasp of the tape playing in her head (below her conscious awareness level) that sets her off and leads to so much pain in the first place. Sue picked a recent incident, one many of us might find innocuous or only mildly annoying at worst, to take a closer look at what feeds her strongly negative overreactions.

The following is Sue's vertical arrow sequence. To give you a feel for how this works, I will type the question that is normally asked without writing it down. When you do the exercise, ask the question in your head, and note it with the little vertical arrow.

## Sue's Vertical Arrow Sequence

- **My target behavior:** Consider the possibility of less devastating explanations when someone says something that upsets me. For this exercise, I will use the incident when the grocery clerk commented the shade I just dyed my hair was different.

- **My negative thought or feeling when I think of performing my target behavior:** I am so upset that all I can think about is how angry and hurt I feel.

- I will ask myself either one or the other of the following two questions:

    - If this idea is true, what would that mean to me?

    - If this idea is true, what about it upsets me?

- **Doing the vertical arrow exercise:**

    - **What is upsetting to me about what he said?** I think he doesn't like the color of my hair.

    - **What does that mean to me if he doesn't like it?** I feel like he thinks I made a stupid choice.

- **What's upsetting about the idea that he thinks I made a stupid choice?** Stupid people make stupid choices.

- **What is upsetting to me about that idea?** He thinks I am stupid.

- **What is upsetting about the idea that the clerk might think I am stupid?** That would be horrible.

- **What does that mean to me that makes it horrible?** It means I don't have the ability or the control to improve myself. What is upsetting about that idea? My life is aimless. Bumbling.

- **What is upsetting about the idea that my life is aimless and bumbling?** (*This is what I mean by a question that sounds silly. You ask it anyway. You don't stop!)*That means I am wasting my life away.

- **What does that mean to me?** It's sad. Depressed. Terrible.

- **What does it mean to me that makes it sad, depressed, and terrible?** I'm a loser.

- **What is upsetting about the idea of being a loser?** I'm stupid. Aimless. Wasting my life.

- **What does that idea of being stupid and wasting my life mean to me?** I have no purpose.

- **What is upsetting about that thought?** I may as well kill myself. (This is Sue's bottom-line catastrophic thought. Now she can stop the exercise.)

What is the value of this? The first thing Sue did was laugh at the absurdity of this scenario. Then she turned quite serious. She thought how a statement by a clerk—whom she did not care about and who did not even say if liked her hair color—could trigger the huge emotional flood of anger and hurt she experienced.

By way of background, I will tell you that Sue came from a family full of chaos. She played parent to her sexually promiscuous, alcoholic, neglectful mother and suffered severe criticism, including being labeled "stupid" whenever she did not know something or disagreed with her negative, demeaning father. Her parents divorced when she was three. Sue's only dream was to survive childhood and become independent as fast as she could, which she did very successfully by the way. However, her out-of-control adolescent years understandably left her with an intense need to control things, have goals, achieve, and, above all, always be in charge of her life.

For Sue, even the slightest perceived criticism or rejection, set off an entire scenario of dire threat that she was stupid, out-of-control, bumbling, and a loser. Ultimately, her life was not worth living. Anyone who believed that would have a huge emotional reaction!

The problem is that Sue had thoughts and feelings wired together unconsciously that do not belong together. We could start with the fact that she gave the power to upset her to a store clerk she barely knew. Let's say he really did hate her hair color. Let's even say many people thought it was awful. Obviously, if they told her so, she might feel a bit bad and might want to consider their input. She might even change the color if she agreed with them. However, choosing an unflattering hair color certainly wouldn't mean Sue is a stupid, bumbling loser. Even more certainly, it doesn't mean she has lost control of her life, will never reach her goals, and may as well kill herself.

As I said, gaining insight into these underground thought-feeling connections will not in and of itself make them instantly disappear. But it sure helps get you focused on what aspect of your thinking you need to work on. When you are sick, your doctor cannot prescribe the right medicine without first accurately diagnosing your problem. In the same vein, you cannot begin healing your psychic ills without knowing exactly what is wrong. That is where the vertical arrow technique is so useful and easy to use anytime you want a clearer understanding of what it is that is making you overreact to some situation. I will give you another example of someone using the vertical arrow technique in order to highlight how useful—and powerful—a tool this really is.

Ari cannot stand his wife June's thirty-year-old son, Dale. Even June acknowledges Dale, though intellectually very bright, is socially insensitive, boorish, and sometimes downright abrasive. But Ari makes matters much worse by confronting Dale during family gatherings or by sitting silently and stewing. Both are obvious to his wife and guaranteed to upset her. In fact, Ari starts cranking himself up with resentment weeks before Dale's holiday visit. By the time Dale arrives, Ari and June have been fighting over the situation and the atmosphere is already tense.

The intensity of his reaction to Dale puzzles Ari. There are other people in his life he does not care for, but nobody elicits the level of reaction in him that Dale does. So, Ari did the vertical arrow technique. Here is what he found:

### Ari's Vertical Arrow Sequence

- **My target behavior:** To react less strongly to Dale both emotionally and in how I behave.
- **My negative thoughts or feelings when I think of performing my target behavior:** I can't let him get away with acting the way he does.
- I will ask myself either one or the other of the following two questions:
    - If this idea is true, what would that mean to me?
    - If this idea is true, what about it upsets me?
- **Doing the vertical arrow exercise:**
    - **What does Dale's behavior mean to me?** He reminds me of my father.
    - **What does that mean to me?** I can't control the scene.
    - **What is upsetting about that?** The situation is out of control. I'll be embarrassed because of others seeing this.
    - **What does it mean to me to have a situation I cannot control?** I should be in control. I should be able to make him see what he does is not right, like a parent.
    - **What does it mean to me that I cannot do that?** His family allowed this. Now it is hopeless. An uncontrolled child controls the group and events.
    - **What does that mean to me?** A lack of respect for me.
    - **What does that mean to me?** It shows the rest of the world I don't get respect as a parent or an elder.

- **What is upsetting about the idea I am not getting respect like a parent or elder?** I haven't established myself as a parent or for guidance.

- **What is upsetting about that if it were true?** I believe I've done the best I can to be a guide for many people. Loss of pride.

- **What is upsetting about that idea?** Pride and respect are the most important components of a person. Without that, it strips the inner being of value.

- **What would that mean to me?** That I have no value. That I am worthless. (Now we are getting to the catastrophic thoughts.)

- **What would it mean to me to have no value? Be worthless?** Then why was I put here? We're here for something.

- **So what would it mean to me to think I had no purpose in being here?** I would have to answer to myself. I'd be saying, "You have failed to establish what your whole life is about—the meaning of my life."

- **What would failing to establish the meaning of my life mean to me?** I'm nothing! Zero. I thought I'd established myself. Zero! (Here is the catastrophic thought. Ari found his bottom line.)

So here again, we go in an instant from an admittedly annoying situation—Dale's unpleasant behavior—to huge underlying connections about pride, respect, control, one's purpose and value in life, and winding up a meaningless zero. No wonder Ari has such huge reactions to Dale. For him, Dale's behavior is not just about Dale. It is a statement about Ari's worth and purpose. Whenever Dale shows up, unbeknownst to Ari's conscious mind, his unconscious or implicit thought process turns it into a test of Ari's value, worth, and respectability. No wonder Ari reacts so strongly. If you thought your self-worth was on the line, wouldn't you? Of course, that is precisely the illogical connection Ari needs to work on severing. Dale's rude behavior has absolutely nothing to do with Ari's worth as a person. Now Ari at least knows what is going on, which empowers him to deal more accurately with these troublesome notions.

What's fascinating is that all this thinking and connecting of one thought to another as well as the connecting of the thoughts to powerful feelings and desires to act can—and does get—triggered instantaneously and unconsciously. Only the triggering event is apparent, not the underlying process. It is easy for people to find themselves distressed, but clueless as to what is really happening. Vertical arrow to the rescue!

Now it is your turn. Follow the steps I have outlined:

## My Vertical Arrow Sequence

1. Complete the following two sentences. Write them at the top of an 8-1/2×11-inch sheet of paper.

    - **My target behavior is:**________________________________
    - **My negative thoughts or feelings when I think of performing my target behavior are:** ________________________________

2. Write down these two questions:

    - The questions I will ask myself:

        - If this idea is true, what would that mean to me?

        - If this idea is true, what about it upsets me?

3. Begin the questioning sequence. Write your responses on the left-hand half of the page.
4. Ask yourself one of the two questions (whichever fits best) about the negative reactions to actually performing your target behavior.
5. Make a little downward arrow on your paper to show you asked.
6. Write your answer.
7. Ask one of the two questions again. This time, ask with regard to the last answer you wrote.
8. Make a vertical arrow.
9. Write your answer to the last question asked.
10. Keep repeating the process. This is most important. (Getting anything out of the exercise depends on many rounds of questioning.)
11. Even when it sounds like a silly question, ask and answer it.
12. If it makes things clearer, when you pose the next question, combine your last answer with some answers that went before.
13. If you press far enough down into your thinking, you will end up with some fairly catastrophic thought. That is when you stop. Do not stop before.

Let's take stock of where we are. In the first step, you selected a target behavior. In the second step, which we just finished, you identified the enemies to change (i.e., sharpening your understanding of the resistant thoughts and feelings that get in the way of you changing from your current ways to your target behavior). We are now ready to move the third step, the things you can do to cope with that resistance and make it easier to implement your desired change.

# 8

## *Stepping on Stage (Act Three)*

### *How to Retrain Your Thinking and Plan Your Practice*

Eliza Doolittle can barely eke a living by selling flowers on the streets of London. Still, she is fully capable of imagining a better life. In fact, the plucky Eliza does a lot more than imagine it. She takes action to make it happen. She knows her street ways and screechy Cockney speech are a permanent barrier to ever getting ahead. But Eliza is as gutsy and determined as her ragged clothes are sooty. Opportunity comes during a sudden rainstorm via a chance encounter with Professor Henry Higgins, the most noted language expert in London. Despite his belittling manner and blistering invective—he calls her a "draggletailed guttersnipe", a "squashed cabbage leaf" and commands her to "stop crooning like a bilious pigeon"—Eliza sees him as her way out of the streets. Screwing up her courage, she turns up uninvited at his house the next day. With her eye squarely on her goal, unwilling to be cowed by his condescending manner, the determined Eliza ultimately convinces Higgins to take her on as his student.

Eliza did it, and so can you. It starts with imagination. I would like you to fire yours up right now. Take a moment, and let your mind's eye picture yourself becoming unstuck by taking action. See yourself starting to do the things you will need to do to transform your life. Making your imagination work for you is an important first step in taking charge of your life and changing it. It is critically important you do that. Your imagination, if misdirected, can keep you a prisoner of your own restrictive thinking for life.

This happens to many people. They develop the habit of letting their imaginations fixate on past failures, negative feelings, cynical thoughts about others, and endless criticism of themselves instead of thinking about where they want to be heading and what they need to do differently. Think of an obese man. He is desperately unhappy, and his weight causes him all sorts of physical and social problems. Now think. Which way would that man be better off? Using his imagination to constantly ruminate about his weight, berate himself for it, and imagine unflattering things that others think? Or picturing the steps he needs to take to start losing weight and imagining himself actually taking those steps? The answer is obvious. Fixating on negative ideas and rehearsing them over and over makes changing yourself much more difficult, sometimes even impossible.

Sadly, for some people, negative thinking has become such a deeply ingrained habit that it now happens automatically, like a reflex. Undoubtedly, you have met someone like that. No matter what comes along, even something good, a committed negative thinker will find a dark side to worry, criticize, get angry, or discouraged about.

Even if you are not a chronically negative thinker, when you set out to change some important personal aspect of yourself, you can expect it will stir up negative reactions in you. Tension, anxiety, depression, feeling bummed out, anger, and irritability are normal reactions people have to the idea of changing themselves. What is likely to be your strongest feeling of all is an active resistance to getting started. That's normal too. Why should you want to do something that isn't going to come that easily?

There is no way to immediately make such negative feelings and resistance to change vanish. Despite their presence, you can do definite things to minimize their interference and move your life forward. That is what the techniques in this book will teach you, how to move yourself forward whether you feel like it or not. For example, I just mentioned the technique of retraining your imagination. Just learning to refocus your imagination on where you want to head and planning how to get there instead of endlessly rehearsing thoughts and images of why you cannot change is a key step forward.

Later, I will have lots more to say about putting your imagination to work for you. Right now, I urge you to force yourself to move forward by trying desirable new behaviors, including the desirable behavior of retraining your imagination. The sooner you take action, the sooner negative feelings and resistance to change will begin fading.

Obviously, you cannot do anything to stop negativity if you do not know it is happening. So an important step in dealing with negativity is learning to pay closer attention to your own thoughts (that is, what is going through your mind), so you can catch yourself if you start down a negative slope. Once you have tuned in to how you think about the prospect of making some personal changes, if you discover your thoughts are largely negative and full of resistance, the next thing you do is actively and self-consciously shift gears. Instead of allowing your mind to continue imagining negative ideas and images, even though in all likelihood it still wants to, you systematically begin thinking about, picturing, and imagining yourself taking constructive steps that will lead to your goal.

Consciously switching your mental thoughts and images around will probably feel odd, awkward, even phony, or not like the real you. That is exactly the point. What you are about is transforming the old "real you" into a newer model, a "real you" who makes you happier. Naturally, as you push yourself to think and act differently, it is going to feel strange, stiff, and contrived. In a word, it will feel unnatural. That's what happens whenever anyone builds a new habit, which is what you are doing here, building a new habit to gradually replace an old one that does not serve you well.

Think back to when you first learned to ride a bike, swim, add numbers, or drive a car. In the beginning, those things felt strange too. But as you kept thinking about and picturing what it was you were trying to accomplish (as opposed to focusing on how much you disliked doing this or all the ways you might fail at it), you got better with practice. Not only did you get better, but doing it began feeling more natural, a part of the real you.

Earlier, I asked you to use your imagination to picture exactly what you want to say and how you want to come across when you practice your target behavior. In that instance, we were using your imagination to focus on what a successful product (that is, a successful outcome) would look like. There is another, even more important use of imagination in transforming some aspect of ourselves. We use imagination to coach ourselves through the process of change. Where outcome is about the finished product, process is about the steps we need to take to get ourselves there.

Professor Shelley Taylor of UCLA did some very interesting research to determine if people are more successful in changing their behavior when they focused on their desired outcome or focused on the process of getting to that desired outcome. For example, an overweight person (Suzie) wants to lose thirty pounds. Is Suzie better off generating a mental image of herself already slim and trim when she gets the urge to overeat, or should Suzie use her imagination to rehearse the process, that is, the steps she would take to lose the weight? Even though it certainly doesn't hurt to have your outcome goal clearly in mind, Dr. Taylor's research shows that people are more successful in achieving their target behavior when they use their imaginations to rehearse the process (that is, the steps they must take to get to the goal).

Why is focusing on the process better than focusing on the outcome? For one thing, as Dr. Taylor points out, you must first determine what the steps are before you can rehearse the steps toward your goal (that is, before you can rehearse the process). Then you must put them in some kind of order or sequence. In other words, focusing on the process forces you to organize to make a plan. A detailed plan for how you are going to get from where you are now at Point A, to where you want to end at Point B, is much more useful than just imagining how you want to be at Point B but without any plan for getting there.

Returning to Suzie's situation, using her imagination to rehearse the outcome might mean picturing herself thirty pounds thinner, slim, and sexy in shorts and clinging T-shirt. Anytime she tries not to overeat, Suzie calls up that image for inspiration. In contrast, the process approach for Suzie means figuring out all the steps she needs to take to control her eating behavior. That might include

- Deciding the types and amounts of food to eat
- Clearing the house of certain foods
- Planning meals
- Shopping for the right foods
- Avoiding specific situations that create too much temptation
- Attending a support group meeting
- Reminding herself that urges are uncomfortable but not dangerous if she does not give in to them

I hope I have made the process versus outcome distinction clear. If so, it is time for you to form your own process plan to help you work step by step toward your goal in a take-charge manner. To recap, in previous sections, you:

- Specified your target behavior, both what you want to say as well as your desired body language and overall manner of how you want to come across
- Brought into conscious awareness unrealistic catastrophic thinking that blocks you from moving forward with the change process
- Committed yourself to the idea that you can—and will—move forward despite negative feelings and resistance that is likely to get aroused within you. You understand these are only feelings, not facts. You understand you can tolerate those unpleasant feelings because they do not pose any realistic threat to your well-being.

With all that in place, you are now ready to create an action plan or what I am calling a process plan.

## Creating Your Process Plan

The steps for generating your personal process plan are simple and straightforward. The key to creating a successful plan is being thorough. Think things through carefully. Try anticipating all the steps needed to get you to your target goal. Review your list. See if you left anything out. If so, add it in.

### My Process Plan

1. On the left-hand side of an 8-1/2×11-inch sheet of paper, write (or type) a list of every step you can think of that you need to take to ensure you get to your target goal.
2. Put the items in your list in a logical, stepwise sequence (that is, the way they would need to take place in real life).

Here is an example: Wayne wants to go to college and get his bachelor's degree, but he has a terrible time getting himself to do the necessary study and homework. Although he was of average ability, when he was a child, his parents pushed him so hard to match the grades of his brainy, older brother that Wayne eventually quit trying at all. By his teens, even though he was heavily into drugs, he managed to scrape through high school and eventually even limped his way through a couple community college classes. However, his grades were low because he had developed neither the attitude nor the study skills to make it as a student. Rather, whenever something is hard to learn or boring, Wayne falls back on his well-developed habit of either avoiding it outright or starting but then quitting at the first feelings of distress. As a result, at the age of thirty, he has had only marginal jobs. He is still financially dependent on his parents. He has enrolled in a math class at a community college as a warm-up to becoming a regular student. Wayne developed a process plan for getting through the course with at least a C grade.

In developing his process plan, Wayne concluded he needed to:

1. Spend one hour a day, five days a week, on homework.

2. Not do the homework at home.

3. Remember he was doing this for himself, not anyone else.

4. Do his homework in the mornings when his energy level was highest.

5. Work in short blocks of time with breaks.

To accomplish these steps, Wayne had to ensure he took other steps. These included:

A. Waking, getting out of bed, eating breakfast, and getting dressed by a certain time to allow time to do the homework.

B. Working at the library because home had too many distractions.

C. Taking breaks every fifteen minutes. Because he smokes, he chose to go outside and have a cigarette or a piece of candy at these breaks.

D. Completing all the homework problems in the unit under study for that day before leaving the library.

E. Checking the answers to the problems where available.

F. Trying to figure out the solutions when he was stuck.

G. Going to the tutoring lab if he did not understand a problem or discussing it with the teacher.

H. Not getting behind for even one day. (For Wayne, in the past, falling behind was a signal he was on the downhill slide. He would say, "Why bother?" Then he would quit.)

I. Start reviewing for tests a week before the test.

J. Understanding the principles behind the problems as well as trying to do the problems correctly.

K. Rewarding himself mentally for his efforts. (Wayne created a list of things he wanted to remember to tell himself, such as "It's hard but I am sticking to it…I do not have to be perfect and get As…I just want to pass with a C or better…This is a learning process…I am learning how to study…")

L. Encouraging himself to keep going by remembering all his reasons for persisting in doing this, such as wanting to be independent, go to school, and have a career.

M. Reminding himself he did not have to follow his feelings and quit doing the homework, even when he strongly wanted to.

Look at steps 1–5 and A–M. It took an impressive amount of thinking and planning for Wayne to make those lists. In contrast to his process plan, an outcome plan would have only had Wayne picturing having somehow successfully completed all the homework, passed the course with a good grade, and feeling wonderful about it. It is just what it says—an outcome—but it does not offer any guidance for how to get yourself from where you are to that outcome. Like Wayne, you need to develop a detailed process plan for yourself. Please do that now.

## Recap

Let's stop for a moment to recap where we are. If you completed all the action items from previous sections, here is what you have accomplished. You have:

- Specified your target behavior, both what you want to say as well as your desired body language and overall manner of how you want to come across

- Brought into conscious awareness unrealistic catastrophic thinking that blocks you from moving forward with the change process

- Committed yourself to the idea that you can—and will—move forward despite negative feelings and resistance that get aroused because they are only feelings, not facts. You understand these negative feelings do not pose realistic dangers to you.

- Made a process plan that shows, step-by-step, the actions you need to take to reach your target goal

Having taken all these steps, you now know what you want to do as well as the catastrophic ideas you used in the past to scare yourself into not doing it. What's more, you also now know that negative feelings that cause you to resist change are to be expected, but you can move forward despite such feelings because they are only unpleasant and uncomfortable, not dangerous or any kind of real threat. Lastly, you have made a detailed list of the steps you need to take to get you from Point A (where you are today) to Point B (where you want to be once you have implemented your target behavior). That all sounds pretty good—and it is—except for one piece that is still missing.

## Take-Charge Thinking: The Stepping Stone to Action

Taking action, as you'll hear me say often throughout this book, is the bottom line of fulfilling take-charge living to transform some aspect of yourself. If Eliza Doolittle had not pushed to get Professor Higgins's help, there would be no Fair Lady, just the same yowling, bedraggled flower seller as when the play opened. That's true for any of us. Without action on our part, there can be no transformation, just a lot of wishful thinking and excuses for remaining stuck doing the same old things.

Taking action involves changing behavior, but there is a better and a worse way to take action. The better way involves changing your thinking patterns, how you mentally talk to yourself, along with changing your behavior. Far less desirable is forcing yourself to behave differently but still hanging on to old, unhelpful ways of thinking. I will give you an example of what I mean.

Joe, a recovering alcoholic, has been sober for three years. Like others in successful recovery, Joe does more than abstain from drinking. He now understands himself better and knows how he used alcohol in the past to numb himself to avoid dealing with his problems, especially to avoid conflict. Along with this new self-understanding, Joe adopted a new philosophy and new thinking about how he wants to live his life.

He summed it up this way, "I have to face issues and deal with them. I've learned I can do that, and I don't have to hide out in a bottle. If it means an argument, I can handle that, too. No more running. No more hiding. No more booze."

That way of thinking helped Joe become a real father to his two sons, finally standing up to his loud, very difficult ex-wife instead of letting her run the show and make decisions he felt were harmful to the boys. A major sea change like that doesn't happen overnight. It takes time and effort. In fact it's an ongoing growth process for Joe. The point I want to highlight is that the critical shift in Joe's thinking about himself and his need for alcohol is what enables Joe not just to abstain from drinking, but to be at peace with not drinking. Thus, Joe is neither a white-knuckler nor a dry drunk.

In case you are not familiar with the terms, white-knucklers give up drinking, but they fail to change their underlying thinking about themselves in relation to booze. So, their belief in their need to drink is never resolved. Each day is like knuckles turning white from clinging to the edge of table, desperately wanting to reach for a drink, battling to resist.

Like white-knucklers, dry drunks are also alcoholics who stop drinking. However, they do not stop the dysfunctional thinking and acting out that got them into trouble when they did drink. Someone like Max, a dry drunk who got into drunken brawls in bars, is still picking fights and getting arrested. Instead of taking an honest look at himself, the way Joe did, Max rages that everyone else is the problem and the world is giving him a raw deal.

What is the difference between a successful, recovering alcoholic like Joe and the white-knucklers and dry drunks? It is not the behavior, at least not as far as drinking goes. All abstain. The difference is what happens inside their heads—their ways of looking at themselves and the world as well as their ways of talking to themselves.

Like Joe, the inner dialogue you have with yourself—consciously or not—is just as important as your outward behavior. Taking charge and transforming your life is not a matter of forcing yourself to act differently while feeling nervous, depressed, enraged, guilty, or otherwise unhappy about doing so. Quite the contrary. Truly taking charge of your life means reorganizing the conversations you have with yourself inside your head so your thinking supports, not obstructs, your new behavior.

## Dumping Dysfunctional Thinking Patterns

The technical name for this process of reshaping your thinking is cognitive (the act of knowing) restructuring (to alter the structure of something). And that's exactly what it is—dismantling old unhelpful ways of thinking about things and replacing them with rebuilt ideas that give you helpful, more realistic ways of assessing yourself and your situation.

I like to use the image of a movie or videotape to explain how cognitive restructuring works. Think of yourself as repeatedly replaying an old, critical, negative, pessimistic tape in your head, probably for years. That tape blocks you from moving yourself forward. With cognitive restructuring, you replace the old tape's story line, the images, and the soundtrack with a new one that is more realistic, constructive, and helpful in reaching your goals.

Contrary to what some of you may be thinking, this new tape you are will construct is not about cheerleading. You are not trying to prop yourself up with the kind of upbeat hype that sounds encouraging, but does not do any good in the long run. Your new mental movie will certainly benefit from positive ideas and images as long as they are realistic, but the critical feature of your cognitive restructuring is learning and practicing how to think non-negatively. Thinking positively and thinking non-negatively can be—but don't have to be—one and the same thing.

Using cognitive restructuring to shift your thinking patterns and remake the movie in your mind is a systematic process that takes a little time along with knowing the correct sequence to follow. As we proceed, I will outline that sequence for you. But first, to get you in the spirit of things, try thinking of yourself as a film editor. Your job is to remove all footage on your current tape in which your role calls for negative, old thinking habits; tired dialogue; and unhelpful ways of acting. In its place, you're going to create and edit in footage of you engaged in dynamic, new ways of thinking, speaking, and acting. Later, I'll guide you through dress rehearsals that will gradually get your real-life behavior to match how you see yourself in your mental movie.

Using cognitive restructuring to help you establish new habits in the way you think and act is a process that takes three things to succeed:

- Time
- Following the correct sequence
- Practice

As you move through the process, be patient with yourself. Remember to pat yourself on the back for the positive efforts you are making to move yourself along the road to change. It also helps to know, when it comes to how humans think, feel, or behave, as a species, we are not hardwired to make important changes very quickly. Understanding that from the start helps keep you from getting discouraged.

## Remaking That Movie in Your Mind

Using the procedures indicated below in parentheses, the actions I have asked you to take so far are:

- Pick a target for change (Checklist 1—My Relationship Roles and Checklist 2—*My Role With Myself)*
- Figure out what thoughts stand in your way of changing (*Vertical Arrow Technique*)
- Lay out your action steps to change (*My Process Plan*)

Those are essential groundwork. We now arrive at the hard-core work of actually producing change in yourself. First, we'll work on changing your thinking. Then we will work to change your behavior. Notice I did not say anything about changing your feelings. Feelings change after thinking and behavior changes, not before. So forget about waiting until you "feel ready" to start. Regardless of how you feel, commit to getting started anyway.

We begin with cognitive restructuring. You can call it thought changing, mind control, making a new mental tape. As I explained earlier, you must work to replace the negative script and tape that runs in your head with a nonnegative one. That takes time and practice. After all, your old script has been around such a long time. It is so well-rehearsed that you could not possibly expect to make it disappear with a snap of your fingers. Then again, most important new things you have learned throughout your life took time and practice.

As you work to change yourself, I guarantee, if you approach the whole process with the right attitude, it helps make things easier and more pleasant for you. Negativity, intolerance, impatience, perfectionism, self-criticism, and procrastination are your enemies. Good cheer, humor, patience, flexibility, willingness to keep plugging, tolerance for mistakes, and lots of pats on the back for effort are your friends. Even go the whole distance and think of learning how to act in this new, take-charge way as an adventure!

Let's start by reviewing the results of two exercises I asked you to complete earlier. Please review these papers to refresh your memory. If you did not do them, do so now.

- The Vertical Arrow Technique

- My Process Plan

The vertical arrow technique reveals scary, catastrophic thoughts you tell yourself that prevent you from going forward with your targeted behavior change. Your process plan, in contrast, lists the positive steps you need to take to move toward your desired behavior. It is a near certainty that you have resistance to taking some of the steps you listed (that is, you have long-standing feelings and reasons why you have not—and maybe thought you could not—take such steps). In that sense, your process plan list shares something in common with your vertical arrow list. For both, thoughts exist in your head that are obstacles to taking needed actions.

On your process plan, review each step. As you do, think about if you have any negative thoughts about performing that step. If so, write the negative thought next to the step. Once you have done that for all the steps, you have, if you look at both your vertical arrow and process plan lists, a comprehensive collection of all your negative, unhelpful, nonconstructive ideas that need cognitive restructuring.

In the past, some of those beliefs may have been operating outside of your awareness. Nonetheless, they affected what you did. Other beliefs you probably knew quite well. Using the vertical arrow and process plan exercises, you now should have a good handle on your key cognitions or beliefs that need of restructuring. Restructuring your beliefs means countering or disputing them with:

- More realistic ideas
- More accurate ideas
- Ideas that are supported by evidence
- Ideas that are constructive and non-negative.

Notice I did not say the ideas must be positive, just nonnegative. In contrast, the beliefs you have been carrying around until now, the ones that unnecessarily prevent you from transforming some aspect of yourself so you can pursue your goals, do tend to be unnecessarily negative assessments of your situation. Unnecessarily negative beliefs are:

- Inaccurate
- Unrealistic
- Not based on good evidence
- Overly self-critical
- Biased towards expecting very unlikely catastrophic results.

Of course, some beliefs that restrain us from taking action are realistic assessments of danger. This book is not about coping with such situations—say leaving a physically abusive spouse. Take-charge living is about changing what is realistically within our power to change without exposing ourselves to undue harm. The famous Serenity Prayer used by many twelve-step self-help groups says it beautifully:

> God grant me the serenity to accept the things
> I cannot change, the courage to change the things
> I can, and the wisdom to know the difference.

The wisdom to know the difference is the key. What prevents people from changing, even when they are firmly convinced they would be better off doing so, is incorrectly believing they are not capable of making the change, or something awful will happen to them if they change. The truth is that they can change with proper guidance. Despite their fears, realistically nothing unmanageable or catastrophic will happen as a result.

The first step of cognitive restructuring is identifying the beliefs causing the problem. The next step is disputing those beliefs. Disputing means raising doubts, challenging, contradicting, and questioning the truth of those beliefs. It also means impugning them by attacking, opposing, contradicting, negating, assailing, and criticizing them.

In principle, disputing sounds good. But who hasn't had the experience of using good arguments in debates with themselves and getting nowhere? Then it's easy to incorrectly conclude that changing your thinking is a good idea, only it can't be done, or at least you can't do it. To counter that idea, you need to understand two of the most important principles about how people change.

First, change requires persistence. After years of silence as a shy person, you cannot simply tell yourself to start talking up at the next staff meeting and expect your old fears to disappear. Rather, you have to come up with good quality evidence and realistic, accurate, non-catastrophic, nonnegative thinking as to why you can and should talk up. Like an actor preparing for opening night, you must rehearse those ideas over and over. Even when you do, you won't truly believe the new ideas at first. Remember, not only have your old ideas been around a while, but they are also hooked to some powerful feelings. It is okay that you cannot emotionally buy into the new ideas. Keep thinking them and trying them out anyway. Little by little, they will take hold.

That brings me to another major principle—the action imperative. Let's say you do a great job with cognitive restructuring. You rehearse the new ideas, you are open to them, and you find they are even sinking in a little. For those new ideas to do you any good, you must follow up your cognitive restructuring with a performance of the new behavior. You must do that in the face of boulder-sized negative feelings that are likely to surface and try manipulating you into believing you cannot—or should not—take a chance on acting differently. This is where some hard work on your part comes in. However strong the feelings trying to stop you, you must force yourself into changing your behavior anyway. Knowing it's normal to feel pulled in opposite directions helps, but committing yourself to act, regardless of how you feel, is what essentially counts. Many people have it backward. They want to feel ready first and then start changing. It doesn't work that way. By letting go of that expectation, you'll save yourself a lot of frustration and disappointment. Accept that forcing yourself to take action, even when that goes against strong (but dysfunctional) feelings to the contrary, is the correct—sometimes the only—way to get yourself on the road to growth.

Transforming your thinking (cognitive restructuring) requires persistence. You must try the new way of thinking, rehearse it, and give it time to attach itself to you. You also have to be willing to buck powerful feelings that tell you that making this personal change is too hard, dangerous, or impossible. Keep reminding yourself that, powerful as they are, these are only feelings, not facts. It's a boulders and BB's problem. The resisting feelings are boulders, big, strong, and solidly grounded. Those newly restructured ideas you are injecting into your brain are BBs. But if you continue tossing those pellet-sized BB's of an idea at the boulder, as well as force yourself to try out your new target behaviors, you will begin chipping away at the negative feelings. Like it or not, that's how human change works. Don't fight it. Don't give up on it. Just understand the process and work with it.

Having said all that, let's get on with the basics of how you actually apply cognitive restructuring to change your thinking. As I said earlier, I like to think of it as replacing an old dysfunctional tape that has been playing in your head with a realistic, nonnegative one designed to empower you to move forward toward your goals. You do that by disputing the unrealistic thinking you have been applying to the situation until now. I will shortly set out a sequence of steps for you to use to dispute your personal dysfunctional beliefs.

Before I do, I want to draw your attention to the nature of the thinking errors that people make that stress their lives and hinder change. By thinking errors, I mean ways of twisting or distorting our thinking so we end up seeing the things other people say or do, and seeing ourselves, in an overly negative, pessimistic and self-demeaning light that has little or no basis in reality—just the sort of thinking in need of cognitive restructuring. The hook in thinking errors is that to us our incorrect beliefs feel true and seem totally realistic, which is why we keep on believing them. In fact, without some cognitive restructuring, people can carry around exaggerated, untrue beliefs about themselves for a lifetime, never questioning if there's any evidence to support them.

Here are seven examples of people making thinking errors along with ways they begin correcting them. See if any of the errors are the types you tend to make. If so, pay particular attention to the corrected thinking. Obviously, thinking a brief corrected thought just once probably won't accomplish much. But if you make a habit of catching yourself and really working at creating a whole script that corrects such errors, over time you will feel better about yourself and less threatened about making changes in your life.

## Seven Scenarios For Tackling Thinking Errors

*1. Dan, an A college student, gets a C on an exam. Dan concludes he is a total failure.*

Dan's corrected thinking is: *"This is only one exam. One exam won't have any real impact on my future. I didn't study enough because I was sick. Usually I do well. There's absolutely no reason to think I won't do well in the future."*

Do You Have An Example From Your Life Where You Go From A Single Negative Experience To Thinking The Worst About Your Whole Life? Write It In:

*2. Sheri is seeking a new romantic relationship. She recently began corresponding via e-mail with a man she met through an Internet dating service. He e-mails her and writes that he misplaced her phone number and asks her to send it again. Sheri is furious. She doesn't believe he lost it. She's sure he is just stalling about calling. She is also insulted that he thinks he could fool her that way.*

Sheri's corrected thinking is: *"Wait a minute. Look at the big picture, Sheri. So far, this man Sam has been very nice in our e-mail correspondence. He hasn't given me one single reason to think he's a liar. Just because that my old boyfriend Ernie used to lie to me, don't confuse Sam with Ernie."*

Do You Have An Example From Your Life Where You Lock Onto One Detail, Misinterpret It and Then Come To An Entirely Wrong Conclusion? Write It In:

*3. Jesse has a low opinion of himself. When anybody pays him a compliment, Jesse thinks one of two things. Either they are just being nice but don't really mean it, or, on the off chance that they do mean it, he has fooled them.*

Jesse's corrected thinking is: *"Could it be that there really are positive things about me that others like? Maybe so. People have no reason to lie to me. Most people have some good qualities. I must too."*

Do You Have An Example From Your Life Where You Discount Positive Things Others Say About You? Write It In:

*4. Janet's husband looks unhappy when he gets home from work. Janet concludes he hates coming home. She thinks he is probably sorry he married her. Then she wonders if he's been fooling around. Thinking this way, Janet becomes silent and withdrawn.*

Janet's corrected thinking is: *"Don't let your mind race. Stop assuming things. Jim's never given me any reason to think he's fooling around. Ask him why he seems so down. Maybe it has nothing to do with me."*

Do You Have An Example From Your Life Where You Automatically Take Things Personally And Assume The Worst? Write It In:

*5. Sy has done fine at his job. But when his boss sent back a report saying it needed revisions, he became very anxious she might fire him. From there Sy's mind raced to thoughts that he would never find another job, his wife would leave him, and he eventually would wind up a bagman!*

Sy's corrected thinking is: *"Hey man, weigh the facts. I have a more than satisfactory work record. My boss Jenny has never given the slightest indication she thinks of firing me. Even if she did, with my skills I could be on another job tomorrow."*

Do You Have An Example From Your Life Where You Find Reasons To Worry About Something Bad Happening Even Though The Event Is Most Unlikely And Does Not Fit The Facts? Write It In:

*6. Alicia feels guilty and thinks she is a bad person because she said something negative about her dead mother to her therapist.*

Alicia's corrected thinking is: *"My mother had emotional problems and was very cruel to me. I feel guilty and like a bad person saying that about her, but it's true. And just because I feel guilty and bad, doesn't mean I should be guilty and I am bad. Those are feelings, not facts, and I want to work on getting rid of them."*

Do You Have An Example From Your Life Where You Believe Your Feelings Even Though The Facts Contradict The Feelings? Write It In:

*7. The teacher wrote Leta that her daughter was not working well in class. Leta jumped to the conclusion that it was her fault and she was a bad mother.*

Leta's corrected thinking is: *"The teacher says my daughter needs a tutor and we arranged it. That has nothing to do with me as a mother. In fact I'm a good mother who supports my daughter's efforts and gets her the help she needs. This isn't about motherhood, it's about me being so ready to blame myself even for problems that aren't about me."*

Do You Have An Example From Your Life Where You Blame Yourself For Things That You Were Not Responsible For? Write It In:

If any of these thinking distortions sound like something you do, work at catching yourself while you're doing it. It takes a little practice because this kind of thinking error often is such a well ingrained habit that it occurs automatically. But when you know what you're looking for, with a little effort you'll be able to tune in. Catching yourself in the act is step one in correcting distorted thinking.

Next, having spotted a piece of distorted thinking, ask yourself what a corrected way of thinking would be. What could you be telling yourself that is more accurate, more realistic, more helpful? Let's say you're a person who doesn't assert yourself much, especially when it comes to requesting things. You want to ask your boss, Linda, for a raise, which you think you deserve. You keep putting it off, fearing Linda will be upset with you for even asking. Corrected thinking could involve a series of questions and ideas that go something like this:

- Is your boss really likely to be upset with you if you ask for a raise? Think about it. You know Linda pretty well. Is she?

- Even if she does react badly, what about her reaction do you think you cannot handle? Think hard. Realistically, isn't it true you can handle it, even though you may not like to? Whatever Linda says, it will not destroy you. You have the right and the freedom to move your life forward. You are not a prisoner. You have options.

- Acting as if you are trapped and have no other choices is just an old habit of yours that keeps you fearful of change and helpless to act. Think hard. You know you are worth the raise. If Linda will not come around (and she is a tightwad with money), what are your other options? Another company perhaps? In fact, one of them tried recruiting you recently. Don't exaggerate your fears about the possibility of a job change as well.

And so it goes. You keep sorting through your thinking, correcting distortions, and drawing on the factual knowledge you have instead of drawing on your emotional fears. As you do, you keep plugging more and more sensible ideas into the equation. What you're doing is teaching yourself to listen to common sense instead of being led around by old, unchallenged feelings and outdated ideas with a track record of holding you back. You're figuring out what some corrected thinking might be, trying it on for size, and giving it serious consideration. As you do, pat yourself on the back for being open and gutsy enough to try a new, much better way of thinking.

Keeping in mind what I have been saying about thinking distortions, let's return to remaking that movie in your mind. As with any movie, you will need to mentally write a script with a dialogue that encourages you and provides good reasons to move toward action on your target behavior. All of us have a voice in our heads that talks to us all day long—self-talk—an inner dialogue. I will show you how to consciously, purposefully take charge of that voice when it comes to pursuing your target goal. You will feel empowered. You will not only understand what's happening inside your head, but you will learn how to steer your thinking in a better direction.

The vertical arrow and process plan exercises should have given you specific thoughts, ideas, and beliefs that hold you back from transforming some important personal aspect of yourself. Now it's time to get down to the business of rewriting your script to counter those ideas. Instead of continuing to let your old tape of overly negative, unrealistic, inaccurate ideas—distortions of reality—keep replaying in your head, you will rewrite the story line of that tape. I will give a sequence to follow to help you along. Once you have a new script, like Eliza or like any actor, you must learn your new dialogue through conscious memorizing and rehearsing. Later, after lots of practice, the dialogue will come more naturally to you. But at this stage, keeping your new dialogue plugged into the movie in your mind is going to take effort. I assure you the result is worth it.

What you say to yourself (your inner dialogue) has everything to do with how you feel about yourself and what actions you are willing to take to reach your goals. You have already brought the negative ideas underlying your dialogue out into the open using the vertical arrow technique. Now we're ready to have you call them into question, raise doubts, challenge, and actively dispute the troublesome notions you've carried around for way too long. We will be retraining your thinking and self-talk to make it more:

- Realistic
- Accurate
- Based on objective evidence
- Non-negative

Active dispute is the right term too. Deeply embedded ideas do not let go easily. So let's focus on yanking them out by the roots. True to form, I have an action sequence for you to follow in which you'll learn how to take each idea or belief that has blocked your progress, and one by one, subject that belief to active dispute. I will lay out the sequence for you first and then illustrate how it works with an example.

## The Active Dispute of Dysfunctional Thinking Technique

1. **What am I saying to myself that prevents me from moving toward my target goal?** Review your vertical arrow record and your process plan. Write your key negative beliefs in the following space. Add more lines if necessary.

Negative Belief 1:______________________________
Negative Belief 2:______________________________
Negative Belief 3:______________________________
Negative Belief 4:______________________________
Negative Belief 5:______________________________
Negative Belief 6:______________________________

2. **One at a time, taking each belief, subject it to the following questions and analysis. (Think out your answers carefully and honestly.)**

Ask yourself this major question: Is my belief accurate? To answer that, ask yourself the following questions:

Might I be overreacting? How?

Might I be using any of the thinking patterns listed in Seven Scenarios For Tackling Thinking Errors? Which ones?

What is my specific distortion?

What evidence am I using to support my belief?

- Is there evidence that my belief may not be true?

After considering all of the above points, decide which you think:

I think my belief is inaccurate.

I think my belief is accurate.

Regardless of whether you rate your belief as accurate or inaccurate, the way you have been responding to it has been getting in your way. That is, you use that belief to stop yourself from pursuing some important life goal. The next section teaches a sequence to help you deal with your beliefs more constructively.

## If You Said Your Belief Is Inaccurate

If you said your belief is inaccurate, that means there is little, incorrect, or no evidence to support it. That is a good insight to have. Still, that insight may not be enough to get you moving toward your goal. The following is a sequence of questions to ask yourself that should help you take charge of the situation by motivating you toward positive action:

- I have decided my belief about what would happen if I acted as I would like to act is inaccurate. Realistically, what in fact is more likely to happen?

- If I still do not like what is realistically likely to happen, what can I do in a constructive, assertive way to prevent that negative result?

- What do I need to tell myself (that is, what script do I need to rehearse in my head) to encourage and motivate myself to take that action?

- What is the worst that could happen if I take that action?

- On a scale from zero to one hundred percent, how likely is the worst to happen?

- If the worst did happen, what things could I do to handle the situation in a constructive, take-charge way? What would I need to tell myself to motivate me to handle it that way?

- Even though I answered the previous questions accurately, am I then undermining or disqualifying my answers by saying, "Yes, but *fill in the blank with the excuse you are using to tell yourself you cannot act*?"

- If you are yes-butting and discounting your answers, return to the very beginning of this exercise. Use it to deal with your "Yes, but" reasons for continuing inaction.

- Give self-praise for sticking with this effort, doing something that is difficult to do (that is, trying to change), being patient with yourself, knowing change does not happen instantly, and, most of all, not giving up.

## If You Said Your Belief Is Accurate

After doing a careful, honest analysis, what if you conclude your reasons for not acting in the past were an accurate belief about some negative outcome occurring? We still need to have you take a closer look at what all that means and examine how you can respond in a constructive, take-charge way that will give you the most favorable results.

Once again, let me say this approach applies only if the negative outcome you fear is not dangerous. If acting would result in physical abuse, possible violence, or other truly dangerous consequences, constructive, take-charge thinking may still be useful, but security and other measures may also need to be in place before acting.

Assuming taking action toward your goal is not dangerous, even though it may certainly feel scary, the following are questions to ask yourself:

1. Even if my belief is accurate, what is the probability, from zero to one hundred percent, that the worst would actually happen? If the chances are very low, consider that going ahead has little risk.

2. If the chances are pretty high that the negative result would happen, ask yourself:

    - What are the implications of that negative result?

    - Is that result as bad as I have been telling myself? Am I distorting how bad a negative result would really be? These questions can help get your fears into a more realistic perspective.

3. After doing 1 and 2 above, proceed to problem-solving. That means taking the following steps:

    - Adopt an overall "taking charge of my life" perspective. That means committing to changing that which is within your power to change, even if your emotions are pulling you in the opposite direction. That also means encouraging and rewarding, not criticizing yourself as you take steps toward changing.

    - Clearly and specifically define your problem.

    - Determine what you have to think and do to solve your problem. Break the big problem into smaller steps you can take one at a time.

    - For each step, think of all possible solutions. Be open to ideas. Be flexible in your thinking. Get ideas from others.

    - Determine what strengths you have for dealing with the problem. Don't be modest. Get an accurate picture of your assets clearly in mind.

    - For each step you need to take, think of resources you can draw upon to help you. Do you need to gather information first? Do you need to make notes or take more time to think things through clearly? Do you need to ask for support from people close to you?

- Be specific. What is each step you will have to take? How will you prepare for that step?

- Think flexibly. Expect to make adjustments in your thinking and behavior as unexpected things occur.

- Have alternative plans in mind in case your first plan does not work out.

- Remind yourself not to distort, exaggerate, or "catastrophize" the dangers or worries associated with taking action.

- Pat yourself on the back for taking charge and moving forward towards your goal. Be especially proud of yourself for doing something that is not easy for you to do.

# 9

# *Hitting the Right Emotional Note (Act Four)*

✦

## *How to Manage Your Feelings When They Resist Change*

### Don't Expect To Feel Like Changing

A fatally flawed piece of reasoning is the obstacle that keeps many people from moving forward with their lives. They quite erroneously believe they must feel ready before they can begin to change their behavior. That is not only wrong. It is exactly backward!

Marta is a good example. At the prestigious New York law firm where she works, Marta is the thirty-five-year-old "whiz-bang" tax expert, an up-and-coming star. Her colleagues would be so surprised if they knew that, outside of work, Marta transforms into a woman so obsessed with her weight that she imagines every stranger passing her on the street reels with disgust as "that fat lady" goes by. To avoid this humiliation, Marta spends most of her free time at home, hibernating and becoming ever more obsessed. Of course, she then overeats and despises herself for it. She wishes for one simple thing of just walking outside and enjoying the fresh air and scenery like everyone else. Occasionally, her friend Ellie tries coaxing her out, arguing, "People are wrapped up in themselves, Marta. They could care less what you weigh!" Marta logically concedes this point, saying, "Yes, I plan to go out. Just not today."

Why not today? Why not any day? Because Marta believes she must feel ready to go out before she can tackle the scary task of walking among strangers. Feeling ready to Marta means losing thirty pounds. Of course, staying home and bingeing all weekend guarantees that won't happen. The mere thought of being seen in public overweight makes her feel so anxious that she never seriously considers leaving home.

Marta is not alone. Lots of people continue doing things that don't work for them, waiting to feel ready before they change and do whatever it is they know would make their life better. The hard reality is this: Humans are hardwired. Our brain wants to see us engage in behavioral change first. Feeling better comes later.

This poses a dilemma for people setting out to change their ways. Why? It is nearly certain they will experience strong feelings telling them they are not ready to make the move. Flying in the face of those feelings—in other words forcing themselves to act contrary to what their feelings are telling them—runs counter to human intuition. It feels wrong. It feels risky. Yet, that is exactly what these people must learn to do, ignore what their feelings tell them and move forward with behavior change anyway. That's what you must learn to do too.

In truth, regardless of how it feels, refusing to let the part of you that never wants to change govern your life is neither wrong nor risky. In fact it's the only way to break out of repeating the same old behavior patterns you know full well are getting you nowhere. You need to understand what's going on when one of these "you can't change" tapes starts playing in your head. More importantly, you need to know what to do about it. Controlling such negative feelings is an acquired skill that takes practice, but it is definitely within your ability to learn. You may never fully be able to trace where your resistance to change comes from. That's okay. What counts most is learning how to manage those feelings. Note I did not say get rid of them. I just said manage them, so you can continue changing your behavior.

Most of us know what personal changes we should and would like to make to bring greater satisfaction and happiness to our lives. But reason, intellect, and our endless New Year's resolutions pale when they hit this wall of deeply conditioned emotions that resist change the minute we move to take action. Those emotions tell us, "We cannot or should not change…The problem is someone else's fault, and they should change, or the granddaddy of all excuses for staying stuck—"I'll (*write that term paper, start my diet, quit vegging out, change jobs, look for a mate, see a doctor about the pain, speak up, apply to school, break off this relationship, be on time*) as soon as I feel ready."

That was Judi's reasoning. She will start the sales report the second she feels better. Never mind it is already 10:00 PM, and the report is due tomorrow.

"Maybe another glass of wine will help," she thinks hopefully.

Let's first take a closer look at what's happening with Marta and Judi, perhaps with you as well. Where is all this resistance to change coming from? After that, we can talk about what to do about it.

A part of you functions like a powerful, but hidden, stage director who lives inside you and orchestrates some of your reactions from below your conscious level of awareness. This Hidden Director (HD), being completely loyal, meticulously follows the life script you spent years writing for yourself. You were not necessarily aware each time you added something to your script, which is why consciously you don't know some of what is written there. Nonetheless, the life experiences you've accumulated over the years and, most importantly, the meaning you've attached to those experiences are part of an inner narrative you've developed about yourself and your life that determines many of your thoughts, feelings, and actions. Your Hidden Director walks around with that script in hand at all times. Depending on the given situation you're in, HD knows which gut feelings, beliefs, and bodily sensations to have your conscious self experience because HD knows exactly which fits your life script. It is like having a play happening within a play. Parts of you operate below the radar screen of awareness, nonetheless influencing how you experience yourself consciously.

Let's say you've been giving a lot of conscious thought to how your life is going and you've decided that your life could and should be better. But you know you'll need to make some important changes (that is, do some things differently) to make that happen. Perhaps you need to speak up more at work, deal differently with your sarcastic mate, or quit smoking. All good ideas, except for one thing—old HD isn't going to like this!

Recall I said Hidden Directors are powerful. So the second you make a move towards change—BAM!—your HD, seeing that this change you have in mind doesn't fit with your old life script, fires a warning shot. Powerful beliefs, sinister feelings rise up in you, telling your brain it's too dangerous, too painful, or flat out impossible for you to move ahead with the change you are planning. So don't even try! Because you do not know everything you have incorporated into your life script, you might not understand what the warning shot is all about. What you will understand though, is an intense feeling warning you against change .

That is what happened to Tori, an attractive twenty-eight-year-old analyst in a government bureau in Washington DC. Since childhood, extreme shyness had plagued Tori. She was not only still a virgin, but she had only been on two dates in her whole life. Still, she dreamed of falling in love, marrying, and raising a family. Her female coworkers kidded her, but only because they really wanted her to find happiness.

"You'll never walk down that aisle unless you learn to say hello first."

Being a good sport, Tori took their kidding so gracefully that her office mate Nan didn't think twice the morning she walked in and said, "Did you see the movie *Chicago* yet? That guy who sang "Mr. Cellophane" reminded me of you."

Tori was aghast! Mr. Cellophane was the ultimate human doormat. She resolved on the spot that she was going to change. Starting that day, she would speak up, express her opinions, and be more sociable, especially around men. Resolute and energized, she spent all day thinking of the things she would say that night when she met a couple of friends for dinner, instead of just listening to them. What's more, at tomorrow's staff meeting, she was going to talk to that nice-looking Dan Phillips, who just joined their unit.

Once Tori was actually sitting at the Paradise Café with her friends, despite the dreaded Mr. Cellophane image, she nodded, smiled, and frowned in all the right places. However, she remained quiet as usual. The same thing happened the next day when she parked herself at the opposite end of the conference table from Dan Phillips and never said a word to him. Given how much Tori truly wanted to change, why?

As soon as Tori felt herself in the real situation getting ready to act (in the café or at the staff meeting), her Hidden Director fired her brain a torrent of incorrect beliefs and unrealistic negative feelings that had been embedded in Tori's life script for years. Not that consciously Tori could have told you many of these ideas and feelings. That doesn't matter. In a flash, Tori's mental radar strongly registered the Hidden Director's message. At the restaurant it was, "I can't speak up. It's too risky. They're all so much smarter than I am. I'm certain to say the wrong thing and sound like an idiot. I'll make a complete fool of myself! I'm lucky they even let me hang out with them."

At the meeting it was, "He'd never be interested in me. I'm so dull and boring. He'd think how pathetic that this chick thinks a guy like him could ever be interested in a drip like me."

It is a play within a play because Tori consciously did not have a clue about most of this underground, emotional cross talk going on between her Hidden Director and her brain. What she did have though, is a powerful gut feeling of extreme risk and danger to her well-being if she risked behaving in a new way. Remember, none of this is accurate about Tori. Feelings are not facts. However, to Tori, it feels true, which, as far as she is concerned, means it is true and that's what she uses to guide her behavior.

That is the dilemma. In the world of successful behavior change, if you wait to feel ready before shedding your troublesome behavior, you are on a road to nowhere. Your feelings will not change until after your brain sees concrete proof it is safe for you to change your behavior. It's a paradox. You want to feel ready before you act, but you must act first to feel ready to do what you have already done! It sounds crazy, but that's the way it is. The only proof your brain will accept that changing is safe, which will allay your old fears of change, is seeing you repeatedly act in a new way. You must *actually change your behavior*;do something that is new and different for you. For Tori, the new and different would be speaking up. Unless your brain sees you act differently, it will continue, just as it has in the past, to listen to your

Hidden Director's warnings that it's too dangerous, too uncomfortable, or simply impossible for you to change your behavior.

The bottom line about making a personal change is that your brain is impressed by, believes in, and acts on two things: what your emotions say is so and how it sees you act.

It does not matter to your brain that your emotions and behaviors are not necessarily an accurate assessment of reality. The brain believes what you feel and what it sees you do. To begin the process of self-transformation, you will need to change how you act. To do that, you will need skills for managing the gut feelings of reluctance or resistance you are likely to experience so you can move ahead with the change. That is what I will teach you next.

Before we continue, I'll say one more time, because it is so critical to your success, it is behavior change—and only behavior change—that impresses your brain and alters the brain's beliefs, convincing it that change is not dangerous or impossible. Over time, it eliminates the negative feelings that made you resist change in the first place.

Of course changing yourself—learning to play a new role in life—needs to be done step-by-step, just as an actor develops a role step-by-step. Before finally stepping on stage in front of an audience, the actor selects a script, memorizes lines, practices at home, and goes to many rehearsals and dress rehearsals. You don't want to overwhelm yourself as you change, so like the actor, you also do it in steps. Ultimately, you must take your new actions into the real world with a live audience. That is, going into action and, after some practice, taking your show on the road is the only way to improve your life.

## Overcoming Resistance to Change Part I: Your Feelings Are Lying to You

How *do* you follow common sense and move your life forward when your guts scream no? The first step is realizing, "Just because something feels true, that doesn't make it true." Feelings are not facts. Feelings are feelings. Our feelings sometimes accurately reflect the facts, but especially in the case of feelings that block you from moving forward with your life, they often do not. Typically, such feelings:

- Are built on a distorted picture reality
- Have never been questioned or tested
- Have no hard evidence to support them

The feelings send you the message that either you aren't capable of making the change, or changing would cause truly awful things to happen—like nobody would like you anymore, or you'd lose your job, or your spouse would leave you, or you'd sound stupid—or (fill in the blank with a catastrophe).

I cannot overemphasize what a breakthrough it is when someone comes to understand that obstructive negative feelings, though compellingly intense, are only feelings, not measures of reality. Having a strong feeling about something does not make what the feeling is telling you true. If your feelings are incorrectly telling you that you cannot or should not do the very thing that would improve your life, you may have to initially struggle to do it, but you do it anyway. As long as there is no objective danger (for example, physical abuse), it is not dangerous to defy those feelings. Defying your own feelings goes directly against gut-level intuition. Once people let that notion sink in and once they get it, they are on their way to changing themselves and taking charge of their lives. It is liberating just to realize, regardless of how compelling your feeling, it does not constitute evidence the message it is sending you is true. Moreover, regardless of how intensely the feeling tells you that you cannot or should not make a change in how you do things, knowing a feeling is just a feeling frees you up to not take that feeling so seriously. Notice I did not say you can make the feeling go away or you can totally ignore it. Instead, you can tolerate the resistant feeling because you do not take its threats as seriously as you did in the past. Most importantly, questioning the accuracy of the threatening feeling makes it easier to move forward with behavior change.

There is a lovely paradox in all this. Earlier, I said two things impress your brain and make your brain believe something. One is the message your emotions send; the other is how the brain sees you act. By not taking your negative emotions so seriously, you are freed up to change your behavior despite those emotions. The behavior change then impresses your brain, especially if you continue repeating the new behavior. Previously, the brain believed your negative emotions, the ones that said it was too dangerous to change. Now, the brain sees proof through your behavior that it is not too dangerous. As that insight feeds back into the system, it gradually saps the old resistance to change of its former power. Surprisingly, as you change your behavior, not only do resistant feelings diminish, but positive feelings about how nice it is to be functioning more effectively and happily actually replace them!

## Part II: Mindfulness, Another Antidote to Resistance to Change

In today's stressful, rushed, high-demand world, people prize being able to juggle many balls at once. Multitasking, flipping from idea to idea, or circling from one task to another, is both expected and valued as a sign of productivity.

I am about to tell you about a very different kind of productivity, one of a much more personal nature and one that is about as far from multitasking as you can get. It is based on mindfulness, a wonderful skill that allows you to relate more productively to your entire world. Acquiring the mindfulness habit is truly a treasure guaranteed to serve you well in many ways.

At a practical level, mindfulness is especially useful for managing inner messages that hinder personal growth. Mindfulness offers you a way to control such troublesome resistant feelings, those inaccurate but intensely compelling feelings I have been talking about, those feelings fighting to keep your Hidden Director wedded to your old, outdated life script, and those feelings insisting you cannot and must not try to do things differently. Armed with mindfulness, you will no longer need to avoid such emotions or escape change. Instead, the energy that went into avoiding change becomes focused on moving ahead. In other words, mindfulness has a direct, practical role to play in helping you successfully make whatever personal transformation you have decided would be good for you, which, of course, is what take-charge living is all about.

Mindfulness can help you with more than simply altering troublesome behavior. It can help you experience many aspects of your life more fully and richly. Despite its heavy-sounding name, once you learn how to switch into the mindfulness mode of thinking, you'll have at your fingertips a refreshing way to give yourself relief from the mental pressures that preoccupy so much of our waking lives. Mindfulness lets you reclaim what children do naturally, see the world through fresh eyes and delight in the wonder of things. I regularly use mindfulness myself.

What exactly is mindfulness? First I'll explain how you do it. Then I'll talk about why and how it works.

In the practice of mindfulness, you intentionally shift your mental focus away from whatever was happening in your mind to observing one single, here-andnow event. The event can be anything, for example, a picture on the wall of the room where you are sitting, a tree along the path where you are walking your dog, people coming and going on the street outside your office, and so forth. For starters you should practice mindfulness by shifting your attention to an external event, that is, something occurring in your environment as opposed to something focused inside you. It is best to start with a simple external event, say observing a tree. As experiencing mindfulness becomes increasingly familiar, pick more complex, but still external, events for practicing. Once you are adept at achieving mindfulness with external events, I will also show you how to use it to focus on and deal with internal feelings.

Regardless of the single event you are focusing on, whether it is simple or complex, external or internal, your first mindfulness step is always careful observation. As you observe the event you selected, be it pleasant, neutral, or uncomfortable, do not try to change a thing. That is very important. You do not analyze, solve problems, make decisions, or plan any actions. You simply stay in the present moment and observe the event.

Next, as you observe the event, use words to silently describe the event and your personal responses to it. Keep your attention completely focused on what you are observing and describing in the moment. Using all your senses, participate actively, giving yourself as rich a description of the experience as possible. Include what the event causes you to see, hear, feel, smell, or taste. Note any other sensations it generates in your body. Concentrate. Do this for two to three minutes at first, longer if you wish. As you become more practiced at it—and yes, mindfulness, like so many other things described in this book, is a skill you must develop through practice—you can lengthen the time you spend being mindful.

Just as important as what you do during mindfulness is what you do not do. Do not elaborate on what you are observing and describing. If you are watching a bird in flight, do not go beyond describing it and spin off into thinking how the bird is so free, you feel like a prisoner in your marriage, you wish you could soar like that, and…No! Just stick with what you see, hear, and experience in the moment—the bird and the sky—the thrill you experience seeing it fly—the warm wind blowing through your hair and across your arms. That is as far as you go when you are doing mindfulness. You do not let your mind wander into associating what you are seeing now with past memories or thoughts about the future. If that does happens, which it sometimes will, do not chastise yourself. Simply gently redirect your attention back to the present event.

Finally, in the practice of mindfulness, do not judge whether what you are observing and describing is ultimately good or bad. Being judgmental is not part of being mindful. Judging can be appropriate if you are problem solving or planning some action. However, mindfulness is only about observing and describing. You do not need to judge anything. Beyond that, when we judge (that is, when we evaluate), we tend to dismiss or avoid things we judge as bad. With mindfulness, the idea is to stick with what you are observing and experience it. If what you are observing feels pleasant, that's easy. If it is unpleasant, you learn to tolerate a negative experience while still observing and describing it. This has important implications for being mindful (just observing and describing) when you are dealing with your feelings and thoughts that are fighting the idea of change.

To sum up, the following are guidelines for what to do when you want to practice mindfulness:

- Observe only one event at a time.
- Concentrate. Keep your attention focused on the event.
- Describe the event to yourself in detail.
- Actively participate. Use all your senses to observe and describe.
- Do not elaborate on the event by associating it with other thoughts.
- If your mind wanders, simply guide it back to the present event.
- Do not judge the event as good or bad. Just observe and describe it.

You are developing and practicing a new skill, so take it in small steps. Start with short practice sessions of a couple minutes and gradually lengthen them. Start with simple events occurring in the environment. I walk my dog in a hillside park every morning. It adds pleasure to start my day by stopping and mindfully observing at least one thing like a berry bush alive with birds or the mist creeping up the mountainside.

As you gain comfort with mindfulness, practice observing more complex events in the environment like things that are moving or changing, such as a busy street scene or a room full of people.

Finally, when you feel really solid with mindfulness, turn your attention to observing and describing your own inner experience of the moment, your feelings and reactions, as well as what is happening in the environment. Mindfulness takes you "out of your head," away from worrying, analyzing, problem solving, planning action, to paying attention, and concentrating to observing, describing, and experiencing without trying to change anything. As the skill of mindfulness becomes part of your life, several good things follow. Attention, concentration, and powers of observation improve. You can stick with troublesome feelings, thoughts, and events you once avoided because your brain finally believes you no longer have to run from them.

Think what a powerful place that is. You are ready to go beyond mindfulness to action, making personal changes you know will make your life happier.

Through mindfulness, you also learn to more fully participate in experiencing your world and yourself. At the same time, you learn to not confuse who and what you are as a person with any particular feelings or thoughts you may be having. This ability to observe and describe your own inner reactions without allowing them to push you around and control you is precisely the power you need to move your life forward.

Finally, there is sheer pleasure to be had through mindfulness. Whether it is listening to music, watching a sunset, feeling a hot shower pulsing on your back, or any of the other million positive life experiences, done the mindful way, you will see, feel, hear, and enjoy them more than you ever did before. Just looking at the sky can be awesome if you observe and describe to yourself how the clouds are moving, the variations in their colors and shapes, and the shadings in the color of the sky. If you're outdoors watching those clouds, observe how the air feels on your face. Is it warm or cold? Is it breezy or still? Note whether the sun is warming one side of your face more than the other.

What gives mindfulness its power? Acquiring the ability to enter a state of mindfulness (that is, learning to participate with awareness and fully attend to and observe and describe one single event) forces you to step back from that event. Stepping back helps you see you as distinct from any given event, even events arising from within you. Mindfulness teaches you to not take your emotions and thoughts so literally and to not confuse your thoughts and feelings about events with events themselves. That is especially important with bad feelings. Say you experience fear. That does not mean whatever kicked off that fear reaction is realistically a threat. "I feel unloved" does not make it a fact that "I am unloved." Feeling unloved may only be my current state of mind. That does not make it an accurate reading of how the world really feels toward me.

In mindfulness mode, you begin seeing an unwanted feeling more as an object you are looking at from a distance, separate from you. The trick is sticking with observing and describing. You no longer let your mind race, starting a chain reaction of negative thinking. The trick is sticking strictly with observing and describing.

I will give you a concrete example from my own life about how things change when you simply observe and describe one single event—in this case a somewhat unpleasant event—without elaborating on it or evaluating it.

Three times a week, I attend an exercise class where we do a lot of stretching and toning bodywork. I dread the thirty repetitions of this one particular leg lift because I build up a lot of pain while doing it. Anticipating that from the start, I track my pain like a hawk. I worry nonstop about how it is getting worse, stress I am nearing the crashing point, and repeat in my head how much I detest this exercise. No surprise that my mental song and dance only compounds my stress, unpleasantness, and dread. However, it never occurred to me that I could think any differently, given the awful pain.

One day, as we were getting into position on our mats for leg lifts, I had a bright idea. I had been teaching myself mindfulness skills. What would happen if I switched into mindfulness mode with the exercise? As we got into it, I purposely focused my attention on the growing pain in my leg. Only now, I simply observed in detail the painful feeling, carefully describing all its aspects to myself. I did not evaluate how awful it felt or how I detested it. I did not elaborate about how I know the pain is bound to get worse, how I maybe will not be able to stand it, how I must stand it because I hate being a quitter, how nobody else has quit and I do not want to be a wimp, how...how...how...I did nothing except pure observation and description of my experience. It was as if someone had thrown a switch! Even though I still felt pain, I also felt oddly detached from it. That detachment, almost like watching my pain in a movie, actually seemed to reduce the pain itself. It is hard to describe, except to say it felt miraculously relieving to put distance between this troublesome event and myself instead of allowing it to engulf me as it always had before.

A key to my success was not evaluating. I had quit the litany of how being in pain is a bad thing and how much I hate this stupid exercise. I am not saying pain is not a bad thing. But no law says I have to keep reminding myself of that! My other key to success was following the mindfulness rule about not elaborating my thoughts (that is, not catapulting myself beyond the immediate moment of merely observing pain into worrying about how it might get worse, how I might reach a breaking point, and how I must not be a quitter). I want to emphasize the power and the benefits of mindfulness come through sticking with only observing and describing. You do no more. You do no less. That puts a powerful tool in your hands for taming negative emotions when they try blocking you from changing your ways.

Here is why I think sticking strictly to observing and describing works. Say the event you are focusing on is negative, for example, my leg pain. By not elaborating on and not evaluating your negative event, you are preventing your mind from leaping to further negative thoughts, which would only deepen how bad you feel. In other words, you are setting limits on what you will allow your mind to experience in connection with the negative event. Those limits slam the door on a cascade of other negative associations that are just itching to join the misery party.

On the other hand, say the event you are focusing on is positive, for example, a beautiful sunset. By sticking strictly to observing and describing the sunset—no leaping to either associated thoughts or distracting thoughts—you do not distract your attention from your experience of the moment. That concentrated attention on this sunset and only this sunset increases the intensity of your focus and, along with it, the intensity of the positive experience.

To sum up, mindfulness gives you greater observational powers, better control of your attention, a sense of clarity as to what is happening, and less fear of experiencing things. That adds up to greater control and empowerment over how you choose to be and live your life. Mindfulness also offers you a quick, easily accessible, nontoxic way to give yourself pleasure breaks from the pressured thinking that consumes so much of people's daily lives.

Back to where we started in this chapter. You cannot wait to feel ready before you set out to change something about yourself. That simply does not work. Instead, you have to learn to tolerate your negative feelings resisting change and move ahead with change anyway. That is not as hard as it might seem. Strongly resistant feeling can be managed. The trick is to first expect you will experience compelling feelings telling you that you cannot change. To understand, just because the feeling tells you something, that does not make what it says true. Feelings are not the same as facts. Feelings are feelings. Period! You do not have to buy into them. When a feeling tries to block you from living a better life, doesn't it make sense not to take its message as fact and to do what you want to do instead?

Once you get that notion—that feelings are not the same as facts—even though that will not make your resistant feelings disappear, you have cut into their power to set limits on you. Coupled with the skill of mindfulness, you now have the needed firepower to distance yourself from forces within you that are resisting change and move forward with constructive action.

# 10

# *How Do You Get to Carnegie Hall? (Act Five)*

✦

## *How to Stage Your Dress Rehearsals at Home*

When Eliza persuades Professor Higgins to take her on as a student, she never dreams it's going to take so much practice—hour after hour, day in and out—to transform from screechy Cockney flower seller to proper-speaking Englishwoman. After a couple months of working at it, exhausted from struggling, there's a scene where Higgins is driving her to repeat her vowels over and over. Near tears, what keeps coming out is, "Ahyee, E, Iyee, Ow, You."

Higgins, nearing his own limits, screams, "Say: A.E. I. O. U!"

"That's what I said," Eliza cries, "Ahyee, E, Iyee, Ow, You."

That's how it is for all of us. Try changing a deeply ingrained personal habit and your old way of doing business keeps insisting itself on you. But like Eliza, if we keep practicing, we do gradually change. Eliza's breakthrough—that famous dramatic moment when she finally gets it—comes during one of their practice sessions. To the utter astonishment of Higgins; his housekeeper; and Colonel Pickering, the linguist with whom Higgins bet he could pass off Eliza as royalty in six months, Eliza, sounding every inch an aristocrat, crisply articulates, "The rain in Spain stays mainly in the plain!"

An unbelieving Higgins has her repeat it a couple times. Triumphant, he cheers, "By George, she's got it! By George, she's got it!"

Like Eliza, it is your turn to go beyond vividly imagining how you want to transform some behavior of your own to actually doing it. Don't panic. We will start you off by practicing in the privacy of your home, following a carefully mapped sequence I will lay out for you. However, like any actor preparing to give a quality performance, you must rehearse and not just once. It should be often enough that you have your words and gestures down pretty much the way you want them. On the other hand, we are not shooting for perfection. Perfectionists are never ready. The goal is simply for you to be reasonably well-rehearsed before going out into the real world for a trial run.

Stick with the following sequence to help you move systematically, stepbystep through your practice sessions. Please, do not rush through the steps. No actor on stage would race through rehearsals and expect to turn out a fine performance. Instead, practice your target behavior the way you intend to do it in real life.

The more realism you can add to the situation, the better, for example, role-playing with a friend. If that is not practical, consider looking at yourself in the mirror as you rehearse your words. I also strongly encourage you to tape-record or even videotape your practice sessions. That provides you with much more reliable feedback than simply trying to remember what you said and how you said it.

## Rehearsing My Target Behavior: A Step-By-Step Checklist

1. What is the target behavior you specified earlier in the book? Write it:

   ______________________________________________

2. Vividly imagine yourself engaging in the desired target behavior. What exactly do you want to say? How do you want to come across in body language when you say it? Keep the following guidelines in mind:

   **Preparing My Verbal Message:**

   - What specifically do I want to say?
   - How can I say it concisely and to the point?
   - How can I say it so I am being clear, specific, and decisive?
   - How can I say it without long-winded explanations, excuses, or inappropriate apologies?

   **Tips For How I Deliver The Message:**

   Make eye contact.

   Keep my posture relaxed.

- Avoid nervous laughter or nervous joking.
- Avoid excessive or unrelated head, hand, and body movements.
- Avoid excessive pauses.
- Avoid hesitancy or stammering.
- Make sure my facial expressions are appropriate to what I am saying (for example, don't smile if I am talking about something serious).
- Have appropriate loudness, tone, and inflection in my voice.
- Avoid whining, pleading, and sarcasm.
- Make sure my voice, posture, and body language are consistent with the verbal part of my message.
- Make sure my voice, posture, and body language are consistent with my outcome goals for the situation.

3. When you imagine engaging in your desired behavior just the way you would like to do it, how tense do you feel on a scale of zero to ten (zero being no tension and ten being maximum tension)? This is called your SUDS level (Subjective Units of Distress). Write your SUDS level:

   ______________________________________________

4. Review the work you did in the previous section using the active dispute technique. That will remind you to avoid distorted, catastrophic thinking. Work at keeping your thinking realistic, accurate, based on objective evidence, and nonnegative.

5. Decide what you want to practice first. Do not attempt to practice doing everything right all at once. Instead, look at item #2 above and pick out one, two, at the most three aspects of your presentation to start with. For example, you may decide to practice the content of what you want to say, plus making eye contact, plus not fidgeting. That's enough for round one.

6. Round One of Practicing Your Target Behavior:

- If you have someone to role-play with, set the scene. Tell the person how to play his or her role. Initially, you may have the person being relatively cooperative at first and then increasing the difficulty of interacting in later rounds.

- If you do not have a partner for role-playing, talk into a mirror.

- Practice a short segment. Just a few sentences will do. Do not allow it to get lengthy. That is very important for analyzing how you are doing.

- **Analysis:** What did you like about what you did in your brief segment? Get feedback from yourself and your role-play partner (if you have one). No criticism is allowed at this point. That is very important. You must first identify all aspects of your performance that went well, even if they were not the things you set out to specifically practice. Of everything you did, some things were okay or even good. It is important to take stock of that. Why? Doing so gets you to notice that some things did go well and sharpens your awareness of your strong points so you can make sure to keep performing that way.

7. Receive suggestions for change for the next round of practice. You go first and then get suggestions from your partner. Note I said suggestions for change. I did not say demands for change, nor did I call it criticism. There is a big psychological difference between the two.

8. What is your SUDS level? Write it: _______________

9. Congratulate yourself for doing this. You deserve it. Change takes work. Self-reward is a critical factor in keeping yourself motivated.

10. Repeat the sequence as often as needed, covering the same or different aspects of your delivery. Work on both what you say and how you say it. As you become more relaxed and more effective, you can make the practice segments longer. You can also make the situation more difficult. Keep noting and writing your SUDS level. As you become more practiced at performing your target behavior, your SUDS level should get lower.

Every step in this sequence has a purpose, so please follow the sequence exactly as written when you practice. As you can see, the sequence starts with specifying a target goal and then imagining yourself doing what you want to do, including exactly what you want to say and how you want to come across in your facial expression, voice, and body language when you say it.

After that comes brief practice segments, identifying only a couple of things to practice at a time. As soon as you complete a short segment, you give yourself positive feedback about anything you did well in that segment, even if it is not what you set out to practice. Most people are very happy to jump on the self-criticism bandwagon. Their first urge after finishing a practice segment is to rattle off everything they did not like about what they did. Do not do that! Negative expectations and self-criticism are what have kept you from changing in the past. Taking note of what you did right (and you did do some things right) is very important. In fact, it is critical to success. Otherwise, you are likely to gloss over your strengths. Highlighting your strengths, not skimming over them, is what you need to do. That sharpens them in your mind to help you make sure to repeat them.

Finally, we move to suggestions for change. I hope you will use the idea embodied in suggestions for change, not only in practice sessions, but also in how you approach life in general. First, you recognize you need to make a change. Then you make a plan. After that, you try new responses. You realistically expect your efforts to be imperfect because you realize you are in the same position as an actor who is just beginning rehearsals. Like that actor, you need feedback from the director about what parts of your performance need improvement. In this case, you are both the actor and the director—Eliza and Higgins—guiding your own transformation. What you do is use what you learn from each round of practice to both fine-tune your performance and become more comfortable with the whole idea of behaving in a new way. Perfectionism and self-criticism are your enemies. Patience and self-praise for effort are your friends.

Throughout your practice sessions, you write your SUDS level from zero (no stress) to ten (maximum stress). Monitoring is very important because it the concrete record of your progress.

After each brief practice round, I asked you to congratulate yourself. If that sounds silly, let me assure you that this is not an idle request. Self-reward, a simple reminder to yourself that it is great you are on the right track, you are putting out this effort when it is not easy, you are moving your life forward, builds confidence, offers encouragement to continue, and simply feels good.

People you admire, who are in charge of their lives and operate confidently, remember to appreciate positive things about themselves. It isn't that they do everything right. However, when they find themselves thinking or acting in ways they don't like, instead of wasting their time focused on self-criticism, the in-charge people take their shortcoming as a challenge, figure out what they can do about it, and get cracking to change.

Repetition is the final step of the rehearsal sequence. You practice little bits of behavior at a time in short segments. As you get better at it and more comfortable, you crank up the level of difficulty. After a while, you may even find yourself a bit bored with practicing your target behaviors. Hey, if you're bored that means you're not nervous! But bored or not, you need to keep practicing until you've got an acceptable—note I did not say perfect, just acceptable—level of performance going.

## Ron's Rehearsals

Ron is a brainy rocket scientist. Unfortunately, his brains have not done him much good in relating to people. Ron tends to be impatient, critical, defensive, sometimes condescending, and so focused on his own perspectives that he rarely validates other people. As a result, though Ron's technical skills are admired, he does not advance as much as he could with his company because many people do not like working with him. For years, Ron tended to blame everyone else when things did not go his way. Finally, a close friend outside of work leveled with him. To Ron's credit, he was not only able to hear the feedback, but he decided to do something about it. The following is Ron's behavior rehearsal sequence, using the numbers in the sequence I spelled out earlier.

1. **Target behavior:** Ron decided to stop responding by defending himself. Instead, he decided to acknowledge what the other person says, not offer unwanted advice, validate the strong points of others' ideas, and offer his own perspective in a more respectful, less condescending manner.

2. Ron was really a novice at all this, so he had to initially work hard to create a picture of how he would act. With some help from his friend, he did it. The following are some highlights from Ron's goals for what he wanted to say and how he wanted to say it:

    - Reflect what the other person says to show I heard and understand it.

    - Ask questions to clarify instead of automatically criticize.

- Praise the strong points.

- Do not automatically tell that person what I think he or she should do.

- Ask first if the other person would like my suggestions.

- Do not automatically contradict the other person or debate with them. Make the conversation more of a true dialogue.

- Stop all sarcasm.

- Take the defensiveness out of my voice. Use a gentler tone.

- Do not rush. Have a more relaxed, unhurried manner to make the other person feel valued and listened to. Sit down. Do not stand in the doorway with my arms crossed.

- Smile more.

- Suggest informal contact like discussing things over lunch.

3. Ron had been defensive for so long and thought of it as such a necessary way to protect his interests that the idea of letting go of it raised a fair amount of anxiety. Ron rated his SUDS level before the first round of practicing as 8.
4. Ron reviewed his active dispute technique papers. I will not go into all the details here, but basically much of his negative thinking revolved around ideas like:

    - If I'm not on guard, other people will try to take advantage.

    - I must show I am right all the time; else, they'll ride roughshod over me.

    - If I don't prove I am right, they won't respect me.

    - I'm smarter than most of them. If they don't want to listen, it's their problem, not mine.

- It's a waste of my time to have to suck up to fools. I just want to get the work done.

5. **Deciding what to practice first:** For his first round of practice, Ron decided to concentrate only on two things: reflecting what the other person said and asking clarifying questions instead of giving unwanted opinions as well as a more relaxed body posture.

6. **Round One of Practice:** Ron's friend agreed to help role-play with him, so he told her how to play the part of his immediate boss. They then role-played about a minute's worth of conversations:

   Friend: I've been talking to the customer, and I think we should go in a different direction from what we agreed on Friday.
   Ron: I totally disagree!
   Friend: Of course you do. So what's new!
   Ron: (*He sits down and tries relaxing his body and facial expression.*) I guess something important must have come up or you wouldn't have changed your mind. What's cooking?
   Friend: They heard about some new developments over at ComCal.
   Ron: (*Gets agitated.*) That bunch of fools!
   Friend: Next round of bidding, our customer is thinking about shifting some of their contracts over there.
   Ron: Wow. That is bad news. What can we do? (As instructed, Ron stopped the practice here, to keep it brief enough to analyze.)

7. **Analysis:** What did Ron like about what he did? Even though his first urge was to criticize himself, Ron stayed with the program of looking for what he did like.

   - He liked that even though he got off on the wrong foot, he remembered to shift gears.

   - He liked that he sat down, he relaxed his body, and he unclenched his jaw, which softened his facial expression.

   - He especially liked that he validated his boss must have had a reason to change his mind and Ron inquired about it. This indicated a cooperative attitude about handling the problem.

8. **Suggestions for change:** Ron wanted to stop automatically disagreeing, especially because he did not have any information about the problem. He also felt his put-down of ComCal was inappropriate and defensive. Ron's friend suggested he try smiling a little. She also suggested not opening with a negative remark. Instead, he should be more genuinely inquiring.

9. **SUDS level:** Ron thought the whole process was interesting. He said his SUDS at the thought of doing his target behaviors again was now about 5.

10. **Self-reward:** Ron came up with several things to say to himself: "I am capable of change. I just have to work at it…It's not easy to break years of doing things the old way, but I'm proud of myself for working at it…I like myself for being willing to take an honest look at my shortcomings and do something about them. It's fun not to feel I must defend myself!"

# 11

## *Taking Your Show on the Road (Act Six)*

✦

### *How to Fine-Tune Your Performance*

Real-world trial runs are much the same as what you were doing during practice sessions. You prepare first. Then you try the new behavior. You keep your expectations realistic. It is unlikely you or anyone else will perform perfectly on the first try, so do not set that as your goal. Your goal is simply to do the best you can. Then see how it goes, fine-tune some more, and try again.

For Eliza's first real-world tryout, Professor Higgins had her join his mother and his mother's friends in her box at the Ascot Horse Race, a stuffy, highbrow affair. Looking quite lovely, Eliza is under strict orders to stick to two subjects: the weather and everyone's health. Things go reasonably well until the race itself. Eliza has a bet on a horse named Dover. At first, she cheers him softly, but, as her excitement mounts, her voice crescendos, drawing condescending looks from nearby spectators.

"Come on Dover, come on!!"

Overcome with excitement, oblivious to her surroundings, one and all are aghast to hear the young woman scream, "Come on Dover!!! Move your bloomin'arse!!!

Admittedly, Eliza has had a major blip, but, even then, most of what she did until that last outcry was fine. Despite her outburst, life went on. She continued refining her speech and manners. She ultimately wowed everyone at an embassy gala.

After any real-world trial run, you take stock of how it went. Just as during the dress rehearsal stage, you first review which parts of your performance went well. It is essential you note all successes, however big or small. This helps you know exactly what to keep doing. Only after a thorough assessment of the positive aspects of your performance do you look at specific aspects of your verbal presentation or your style of presentation you would like to present differently in the future. You then do more dress rehearsal work, exactly as described in the previous section. The dress rehearsal is where you smooth out and fine-tune your performance. Then you are ready to return into the world and practice more out there.

Obviously, trying your target behavior in the real world is not the same as practicing it in the privacy of your home. Like everything else, if you get out there with the right attitude and realistic expectations, that makes working on personal transformations a lot easier. I will discuss in some detail several things you can do to help ease the transition from home practice to practice in the outside world.

Note I am still calling it practice because that is exactly what you are doing, practicing new skills and continuing to refine your performance and skill level. Eventually, you will get to a point where your new behavior is so well learned that it feels like a natural part of you. At the trial run stage, it feels anything but natural. How could something you have not done before, something that is not easy for you to do, possibly feel natural? It couldn't. So don't expect it to feel anymore natural than riding a bike or driving a car when you were first learning. Learning a new personal behavior is no different than learning a new physical one. Seven things that will help you along are:

1. Maintaining accurate expectations
2. Dealing constructively with added emotional and physical arousal
3. Converting a threat to a challenge
4. Going from the easy to the hard in small steps
5. Repetition
6. Hooking to higher order values
7. Assuming a take-charge perspective

I will discuss each in turn. Some of what I will be saying, I have said before. However, it is good to remind yourself of these key areas as you set out to do real-world trial runs with your target behavior.

## Maintaining Accurate Expectations

I have said it so often throughout this book. Change is not a single event. It is a learning process. As such, changing yourself (that is, personal transformation) takes time, planning, effort, and practice. So please, park any perfectionist tendencies you have at the door. This is going to be trial and error learning.

For those of you who tend to be overly self-critical, please park that at the door as well. Learning to perform your target behavior is just that. Learning. It is unreasonable and self-defeating to expect a polished performance. What you should expect from yourself is to come well rehearsed for your trial runs. But even with the best of preparation, many factors can influence how that trial run plays out. The idea is for you to get in there and start pitching, to begin moving yourself in the direction you want to go. As you do so, you must be patient, tolerant, and supportive with yourself. Otherwise, you will not want to continue the change process. What's more, learning to treat yourself with support, patience, tolerance, and encouragement is a habit worth developing beyond changing any specific behavior. It makes for living a more empowered and, overall, more effective life.

## Dealing Constructively with Added Emotional and Physical Arousal

When you first get ready to try your new ways of acting in the outside world, you're likely to feel emotionally tense. If you get physical symptoms when you are tense (for example, shortness of breath, knots in your stomach, or headaches), you might experience those as well. The tension is because you are about to do something that is not yet comfortable or familiar. On top of that, you don't know exactly how others will react to your change of behavior.

Such tension is normal and natural. A certain amount of tension is inevitable when people try to transform how they act. The trick is to not let tension, nervousness, feeling down, or any other emotion or reaction hold you back from starting the change process. I have said it before, but it bears repeating. Behavior changes first. Then a change in feelings follows, not the other way around. Don't fall into the trap of waiting to feel ready before you get going.

What can you do about feeling tense, afraid, or not wanting to get started? Unfortunately, I have no magic pills or silver bullets. But I do know some things that help. First, just knowing tension is part of the deal should help. It is certainly no fun to feel that way, but being uptight doesn't signal anything bad. Tension is not dangerous. It's just unpleasant. What great actor isn't tense walking on stage to face that live audience? Just like an actor, you can be tense and still get out there to perform the behaviors you have been rehearsing at home.

Accept the fact that starting to put your target behavior into practice might put you on edge. If that happens, remind yourself that this is a normal part of the deal and you are strong enough to tolerate such discomfort and keep moving forward anyway. Above all, realize your tension is actually a positive sign that you are on the road to self-transformation. You are tense because you are taking action. Think about that. Tension, a case of "nerves", those are positive signals that you're in gear and moving ahead. You are taking charge of changing your life in some way you have decided is in your best interest. That's hot stuff! Really it is!

## Converting a Threat to a Challenge

In every situation, you have choices about how you respond. Even if there is nothing you can do about the external situation, your internal reactions are still a matter of choice. I realize it often doesn't feel like a choice. We all do so many things so automatically, out of habit. Choice just doesn't seem to be part of the picture. Just because it doesn't seem so, doesn't make it so. Just because you're used to reacting a certain way, doesn't mean you must be a prisoner of that reaction for the rest of your life. The reality is that you can choose to start thinking and reacting differently at any time. Of course, that's likely to require some practice on your part, but that's a choice you're free to make.

Especially when it comes to pursuing personal change, which, of course, is what this book is about, a very basic, important choice is the attitude you adopt about the very idea of changing yourself. It may surprise you to realize even the way you approach the self-transformation process is your choice. You can do it with constructive expectations, patience, humor, encouragement, and supporting yourself all along the way. Or you can approach the idea of transforming something about yourself as a struggle, keep questioning your abilities, expect limited or no success, and keep wondering if you should scrap the whole idea.

As I said before, when people go forth to try their target behavior in the outside world, they are often in a state of heightened tension and negative emotional and physical arousal. So it wouldn't be very hard for your thinking to head down a slippery slope of negativity, especially if you're someone who tends toward pessimistic thinking in the first place. "I can't do this…I'm a loser…It won't work…I've tried before…It's not meant to be…It's my personality to be the way I am. There's nothing I can do about that." And on and on. The list of negative things we can create to tell ourselves is endless unless we decide to not say negative things at all. Or at least, if negative thoughts pop into our head, not focus on them, not keep repeating them.

What alternative do you have? Acknowledge what you are doing is hard work and stressful, but frame it in your mind as a challenge instead of a nightmare, struggle, or impending disaster. Moreover, it is a challenge. Challenge implies work and effort, but it also implies you are moving yourself in a positive direction toward a change of your choice and, along with that, comes growth, greater personal freedom, and life satisfaction.

Which do you think is most helpful? Trying to change yourself while playing a looping "I'll never be able to do this" tape in your head? Or seeing yourself as someone who is willing to rise to a challenge, feeling proud of that, knowing you will persist even when it is not easy? People who decide to think about a difficult task as a challenge are people who choose to think constructively and optimistically. Try it, even if you don't normally think that way. Personal empowerment and taking charge of your life is all about choosing how you will respond to things. Helene's story is an example of what I mean.

My friend Helene's mother died a couple years ago. Her ninety-one-year-old father, Julius, an extraordinarily wise man who was loved and admired by everyone who knew him, was diagnosed with lung cancer some months later. Helene invited Julius to move across country to live with her, which he gratefully did. The doctors eradicated the cancer. For a while, things seemed all right, but forty radiation treatments had taken their toll on his lungs, resulting in a series of hospitalizations for pneumonia. Eventually, the doctor indicated it was a matter of months. Julius grew weaker, needing oxygen at home, then a wheelchair, and finally was bedridden.

It goes without saying that Helene's life was highly stressed, especially in the later months. Handling Julius's demanding home care would have been a job in itself, but Helene had to continue running her successful consulting business as well. She had a terrible time finding a caregiver to hire a few hours per week so she could even leave the house. Home or away, every waking hour was burdened, knowing the father she loved so dearly was slipping away. With all her stress, sadness, and exhaustion in those last days, Helene could easily have sunk into a state of pure misery. What kept her from that was viewing this time of their lives together as a challenge and a gift—an experience that was helping deepen her understanding of life and its passing—as well as deepen her understanding of herself. She had never before been alone for any extended period with her father. His living with her gave new dimension to their relationship. It was a wonderful opportunity to watch the grace with which Julius responded to his situation, be good-spirited and devoted with him, and grow wiser for being around him.

Helene consciously chose to look at her situation this way. Another person might have chosen to experience only the stress and misery of it. That is my point. We make these choices, whether we are aware of doing so or not. Looking back, thinking a lot about her father, Helene is pleased with herself for how she chose to handle things.

As you set out to try your new behavior in the outside world, I urge you to adopt my friend Helene's strategy. Think of transforming how you behave as a challenge rather than a struggle. Like Helene, you will find doing that a most worthwhile choice.

## From Easy to Hard in Small Steps

Going forward with practicing your target behavior in the outside world does not mean you must jump in at the deep end of the pool. In fact, that's usually a bad strategy. You don't want to overwhelm yourself. You just want to get started and keep moving in the right direction. It makes more sense to enter at the shallow end of the pool and slowly move into deeper waters as your swimming improves. The general guidelines are:

- Move forward in stepwise fashion, taking small steps if necessary
- Go from easier to harder situations as your skill level and confidence increase.

Remember Juliette, whose immediate target behavior was to relate more assertively to her sister? Specifically, Juliette's goals included being more talkative when dining with her sister and friends, telling her sister not to harp on things like Juliette's refusal to join her on vacation when she knew Juliette could not afford the time off work, and confronting the way the sister talked to Juliette in a condescending voice as if she was a child. Easier to harder for Juliette meant starting with talking up at dinner. The harping she saw as medium difficulty. Addressing the sister's condescending tone and manner was the deep end of the pool, very scary for Juliette.

Juliette started her real-world trial runs with speaking up at dinner. Wisely, she did not set herself the goal of being a fascinating, dynamic conversationalist all evening. Instead, Juliette followed the guideline of moving stepwise and taking small steps if necessary. For the first dinner, her goal was simply breaking her usual silence. She decided to do that by offering at least one comment on each topic the group brought up. At subsequent dinners, as Juliette became increasingly adept and confident, she moved to offering topics of her own for discussion. Then she began directly expressing stronger opinions. After a while, she openly disagreed with some of her sister's opinions. Each dinner provided Juliette with an opportunity to practice and take stock of how she did afterwards. She would determine what she did well and what she would like to change. After that, it was back to another dinner for more practice.

## Repetition

Very few, other than the simplest of things involve one-shot learning. Schoolwork requires study. Sports require practice. A new job means weeks, months, and sometimes years of on-the-job learning. Learning to drive, fly, run Microsoft Windows, bake a cake, or you name it. Chances are, whatever you named took repeated effort. You first just tried to get the hang of it and then tried to get any good at it.

Pause for a moment to think about what is involved when we learn something. We often read, listen to, or watch someone else first. Then at some point we take a crack at it. Whatever we are trying to learn, our first attempts are usually not very good, and nobody expects them to be. However, we keep trying. With each round, we learn a little bit more. Mentally, we keep track of progress. What have we learned? What do we still need to learn? Then we practice more. With enough practice, chances are good we can work ourselves up to an acceptable level of competence or even expertise.

Why do smart, experienced learners think, when it comes to changing themselves, it should be any different? Yet people do. They want personal change (we are often talking about transforming deeply ingrained thinking habits and behavior patterns) to come easily, quickly, not demand a lot of practice, and not make them feel uncomfortable. Well, as Eliza would say, wouldn't that be loverly? It is simply not the way people work. Changing yourself is a double process. Old habits must be unlearned at the same time you learn new habits to replace them. Of course, anything that complicated will take practice. Lots of practice.

Having realistic expectations that you're going to have to practice, fine tune, and then practice some more, will help you move towards your target changes without getting unduly discouraged or worse, throwing in the towel.

## Hooking to Higher Order Values

Think of something that is a very motivating force in your life—your children, your health and your family's health, religious beliefs, political values, environmental concerns—just to suggest a few possibilities. Can you see a way to link your target behavior to that motivating force? If you can, the change you are trying to make in yourself will get a serious boost because the new learning, your target behavior, is not yet a well-established part of you.

In fact, it is a BB-sized little pellet that is likely to be struggling against some strong, well-established feelings that are resisting change. It is our "boulders and BBs" problem again.

If you can hook the change in behavior that you are after to some positive, boulder-sized belief that is already part of you, the new goal inherits added power. It does not become a boulder, but at least hooking up with a boulder helps it grow from a pebble to a respectably sized rock. Give this idea your serious consideration. How might some value you already believe in and hold dear connect in a positive way to the new changes you wish to make in yourself? An example will help clarify what I mean.

Before her marriage, people saw Lila, an attractive, successful Los Angeles attorney of thirty, as socially confident and sexually sophisticated. Lila saw herself that way as well. Three years later, when her husband left her for another woman, Lila's confidence in herself as a romantic partner was utterly shattered. Neither time nor Lila did anything to heal the wound. Instead, she buried herself in raising her twins, Debbie and Don. Friends initially urged Lila to date and get a life apart from her children. Lila always had an excuse why she couldn't. She would have loved a wonderful man to knock on her front door and sweep her off her feet, but she wasn't about to go look for him.

When her children became older, they also began urging their mother to get a boyfriend and maybe even remarry some day. Nothing, not even her adored children, could persuade Lila to take a risk on romance again, even though, in her secret heart, she would have liked nothing better than a loving partner.

As a separate matter, Lila valued independence and strongly believed, if at all possible, children should go away to college as an important stepping-stone to adult independence. That had always been their family plan. Toward that end, she had worked hard and put away enough money for top schools. Both Don and Debbie did well academically. By the time they were applying to colleges, their sights were realistically set on Ivy League schools. Lila got quite a shock when she returned home unexpectedly one day to pick up a forgotten file. From the kitchen, she heard Don and Debbie arguing which story would work best to convince her to let them live at home and attend a local college. It blew Lila's mind. Her kids were so worried about her living alone and feeling lonely and abandoned that they thought they had to sacrifice themselves. Lila decided on the spot that things had to change, and they had to change now.

Lila tied her target behavior (the thing she always wanted but so feared doing, dating in the hopes of eventually finding a life partner) to her higher order belief and deeply held conviction that her children needed to spend their college years away from home. Only actions, not intellectual conversation, would convince Debbie and Don it was okay for them to go. Spurred by that thought, after fourteen years as a romantic recluse, Lila geared up for change. She let friends know of her interest in dating and joined a dating service. Indeed, she even had a potentially serious relationship budding within a few months.

As you gear up for change, I urge you to follow Lila's lead. Review your most dearly held values. Which ones could you wire to your new action goal? Think about it. Then do it.

## Assuming a Take-Charge Perspective

When all is said and done, what helps most in putting your target behavior into practice in the real world is buying into the idea that you have the right to take charge and be the decision-maker for your own life. You can—and should and will—stop giving over to other people the power to govern your feelings, thoughts, and actions, instead of taking that power unto yourself.

After that, it is a matter of doing all the things I've been talking about, for example, coaching yourself through repeated tries at performing your target behavior, using constructive self-talk, avoiding perfectionism, knowing you will have resistant feelings to changing but doing it anyway, rewarding yourself for your efforts, using each attempt to gather feedback for yourself about what you did right and what you want to change the next time, and knowing change takes effort and lots of practice and persisting. If you do all that, you are well on the road to transforming your self and your life.

# PART III
# Backstage

*Securing the Transformation*

# 12

## *Dropping the Curtain*

✦

### *How to Face Your Negative Assumptions*

Rosalia, a nice-looking, forty-five-year-old Hispanic woman, was the youngest of four siblings. She also had the darkest complexion in her family. Growing up, Rosalia's mother, who placed great value on light skin, favored her other children, often resentfully telling Rosalia, "You're the ugliest of my children." So it's no surprise that Rosalia grew up feeling both unattractive and unlovable. As a result, Rosalia has spent most of her adult life tied up in knots trying to please others while ignoring her own needs. The truth of the matter, as anybody who knows her will tell you, is that Rosalia is neither ugly nor unlovable. However, Rosalia's assumption that what her mother said was true has kept Rosalia mired in a joyless life these forty-five years.

When an actor in rehearsal is not getting the part right, the director pushes the actor to reframe his or her picture of the character, see its possibilities in a new light, and deliver a different interpretation of the role. Rosalia also had to go through a process of letting go of her limit-setting image of herself and creating a new, life-enhancing interpretation of who she was. Before she could do that, because her mind was so set on the unlovable, ugly ducking picture of herself, she first had to be convinced that changing her view was even remotely possible and worth trying.

The same is true for you. Believing you can change is critical to actually changing. Some people look forward to transforming something about themselves, viewing it as a challenge as well as an opportunity. Those people are in good shape. If that's you, that's great. In case it's not, let's take a look at people with the opposite view. Like Rosalia, many people assume—quite incorrectly—that they cannot do much about who they are or how they live their lives. Naturally, people who believes they're stuck with things as they are will not attempt to make any changes. In essence, it is a self-fulfilling prophecy. They think they are stuck, so they do nothing and remain stuck. Beliefs like that often get their start in childhood.

As we all know, experiences during those growing up years have a huge impact in shaping who we turn out to be. Many of the feelings and beliefs about ourselves and the world that we carry around as adults have their roots in things we learned as children. Such early learning, especially when it is about yourself, can be very powerful and hard to unlearn, even if it's making your life miserable. Why?

As a child you're totally dependent for survival upon your caretakers. People with that much power, people whose point of view you must hear repeatedly, assume enormous importance. They are your authorities. Because you, as a child, have nothing with which to compare your world of experiences, you assume life, as you know it (be it good or bad) is pretty much how it is for everyone. That makes sense. You really don't know what happens in other families or how other people might think and act differently from the folks who are raising you. Even if you had more exposure and information, your child's brain, with its limited reasoning capacity, wouldn't know what to make of it.

Given all these things (a child's utter dependency, repeatedly being taught certain things and treated certain ways by the authority figures who govern your life, a lack of alternative information, and a limited ability to reason for yourself), it is easy to see why whatever lessons (good or bad, right or wrong) your early world taught you were deeply believable and powerfully implanted in you. Why wouldn't they be deeply believable when that is all you knew? That is especially true of things you were told about yourself. Such notions are taken in and incorporated into your self-image without benefit of alternate perspectives or contradictory points of view. If we are lucky, the ideas and beliefs we learn about ourselves are mostly constructive and confidence building. As adults, we don't need or want to change them. They are the building blocks for continued growth.

But what about the children—sadly, too many children—who grow up in unsupportive, confidence-crushing or otherwise stressful environments? Given how mentally, physically, and emotionally dependent we are as children, if we grow up hearing negative messages about ourselves from the very people we depend on for survival, why wouldn't we believe them? We haven't yet learned to think for ourselves. We don't understand what they say may not be true. Little wonder such early negative beliefs get deeply rooted and resistant to change. If you or someone you love has spent years thinking about yourself in ways that constrict you, limit your choices, and reduce your personal happiness, obviously changing your thinking makes good sense. But as I've been saying all along, we all know from personal experience that changing ourselves is not a snap-of-your-fingers matter.

I wrote this chapter for readers who have been following the plan in this book, working on changing, and finding themselves unable to give it full throttle. If you are like that, I bet you're carrying around some underlying false assumptions. You may not even be aware of them, and that is what is getting in your way of changing. The bottom line of such false assumptions is that they lead you to the conclusion that you are stuck with things as they are. Change, for whatever reason, is not in the cards for you.

Let's take a closer look at this notion of false assumptions. The dictionary says an assumption is when you take something for granted without proof. An assumption is neither a truth nor a fact. An assumption about yourself is simply an idea that, for one reason or another, you've come to believe. An assumption may be true, but true assumptions are not the problem here. The big blocks to changing ourselves are false assumptions, beliefs without any hard evidence behind them to back them up. Don't get me wrong. I'm not putting you or anyone else down for having false assumptions. You came by your assumptions about yourself honestly. Very likely, you learned them early in life. However, making personal changes becomes so much easier once you learn to recognize when you are operating based on a false assumption and stop treating that assumption as a truth.

Of course, some things we believe about ourselves are known to be true. Those things are based on facts, that is, there is solid evidence to back them up. Other things we believe about ourselves—our false assumptions—are not true. They're based on feelings, beliefs, magical thinking, whatever—but not facts. Only they feel true. That's why we believe them. Keep in mind, a false assumption based on a feeling, however strong that feeling, is not a fact. It is still just a feeling.

False assumptions (that is, assumptions without adequate evidence to support them) people make that block them from changing boil down to one of four beliefs:

- Change is impossible for me. Period!

- Change is possible in principle, but I must feel ready before I can start.

- I'm able to change, but the fallout it would cause is too horrendous. It's the other guy who needs to change, not me.

Let's take the first one, the idea that for me, change is impossible. When you propose they make a change, people who believe that say things like, "Hey, look. I am who I am. That's my personality. That's just how it is.

Nothing I can do about that." For most people, that's a false assumption. Not only can they change, they have done so in the past. Only they don't think of that. A "that's just the way I am" person believes their personality is set, their behavior hard-wired into their genes, and that's that!

The next group, the one that buys that change is theoretically possible, has all sorts of reasons why they still can't make the change, or at least not right now. The widow who would like to meet a man but is afraid to look says she will start dating just as soon as she drops thirty pounds. The man who has known about his wife's affair for six months and threatens to leave if she does not stop but is so fearful of going on his own that despite his humiliation, hurt, and rejection, he takes no action. The woman with blood in her stool who does not make an appointment with her doctor, fearing what the doctor might say. The fact is, if each of these people took action now, they could handle the associated discomfort. But their false assumption is that they can't.

Then we have the people who believe changing would produce much more catastrophic reactions than is really the case. The mousy woman who believes if she ever dared express disagreement, other people would have nothing more to do with her. The insecure programmer who puts up with an impossible boss, believing if he quit, not only would nobody ever hire him again, he'd end up destitute, a bag man on the streets.

The fourth group I will note just briefly because they are not likely to be reading this book or trying to change anything about themselves. They are the road rage type. There is no need to examine the assumptions they live by. They are positive their assumptions are correct. What they do is right. Other people keep screwing things up.

It's time now for us to turn the spotlight on you. Let's get specific. Stop and think about it. What assumptions do you make about how assertive you can be? How empowered you can be? Or, asking it the other way, how helpless do you assume you have to be? What limits have you set on yourself that prevent you from changing? Do you assume you wouldn't be able to tolerate what it might feel like to put yourself through a change process? Do you assume the worst will befall you if you speak up, stand up for yourself, or stop letting others run your life?

Too many people severely limit their lives because of these kinds of false assumptions they carry around about themselves. In fact, they could be more self-empowered than they assume. The trick is to not cave in to negative assumptions, but instead challenge them to determine if they are true or false. Please give serious consideration to that thought. Ask yourself:

- What limitations have I set on myself, perhaps without even realizing it?

- What assumptions am I making about myself that lead me to these limitations?

- What hard-core evidence—not mere beliefs, but hard-core evidence—do I have that my assumptions are correct?

- What might be an alternative way to think about my situation? How can I realistically assess what personal change is possible?

- If I discover I have been operating on a false assumption, am I willing to change my behavior, even if doing that makes me uncomfortable at first?

To elaborate on this idea of false assumptions, let me tell you about Charles, a bright, attractive, single, thirty-nine-year-old stockbroker. Over the years, Charles has had so many sexual conquests with beautiful women that he has lost count. A pro at saying all the right things over a romantic dinner and working his dates into bed by the end of an evening, everything Charles utters is designed for sexual conquest. That is because Charles needs to prove to himself, time and again, that women want him and they will not reject or abandon him. The older he gets, the emptier the game gets. No amount of success eliminates his nagging loneliness.

Charles is an example of a person acting not in an empowered way out of choice, but compulsively. He is not so different from someone who compulsively washes his hands or steps over cracks in the sidewalk. Charles does that because of some false assumptions he has made about himself and life. Without detailing too much of Charles's life history, I will tell you that his mother was a very attacking, often emotionally out-of-control person. She was also very demeaning about men. As a boy, Charles quickly learned that trying to express his own feelings or needs only brought down her wrath. Anxious she could abandon him—which wasn't a totally unrealistic fear—Charles taught himself to say and do whatever it took to keep his mother in control as much as possible. That was a good idea, given his dependence on her for his survival. Overall, she let Charles know his mere existence was an unfair burden on her life, not to mention he was, even worse, a male.

Charles grew to adulthood feeling, although he did not know exactly why, he was somehow a bad, tainted person. He also came to adulthood falsely assuming all women and their emotions are dangerous, just like his mother. That made it essential that he remain in full control of any situation involving them. Therefore, Charles never revealed his real self. He was never going to become that vulnerable and lose control of the situation.

The women he dated did not realize Charles was much different than his manner and words implied. Nor could they know, from the outset, there was no possibility of a real relationship developing. Once the conquest had been established, Charles had to move on after a few dates and compulsively play out his seduction scenario with someone new.

Challenging his assumptions was not easy for Charles. Could he really risk being open and honest with women? Weren't most women dangerous as he always assumed? Say he opened up and a woman then rejected him. Could he just cope with that instead of acting as if his mother was rejecting and abandoning him? Was there the possibility something good could come of seeking out the kind of woman he truly admired and being straight with her? Could it be there was no hard evidence that, at the core, he was really a bad or tainted person?

Charles' entire adult strategy in relating to women was based on false assumptions that had no evidence to support them in the real world. It was only in Charles's head. Not all women are like his mother. It would not be the end of the world if a woman rejected him. Although he might feel hurt, he could handle it. He was unnecessarily missing out on the pleasures of real intimacy. Nothing about him would suggest he is a bad or tainted man. However, Charles was so used to automatically thinking this way that he really had to work at challenging his thinking. He did though. And so can you.

Start by closely examining all the assumptions you make about yourself that essentially constitute roadblocks to thinking and acting in the ways you would like. Then take the first step toward taking charge of your life by challenging those assumptions. Are they really true assumptions? Be honest. Are they? Or are they merely ideas you have believed for so long that they feel true? What facts back up your assumptions? Are there other facts you are ignoring that would tend to prove your assumptions are wrong? Distinguish mere beliefs from facts. Challenge the limits you have imposed on yourself, perhaps without even being aware of it. Open up your mind. Think about your potential in new ways. Stop automatically concluding you cannot change when the truth is that most people, you included, can change if they set their mind to doing it. Changing may not be initially comfortable, but you can tolerate some discomfort. It is not dangerous, only unpleasant. And it will not last forever.

Challenging old assumptions is like everything else I have told you about the change process. It takes time, effort, and practice. Be patient, and keep your sense of humor. Above all, give it the serious attention and effort it deserves.

# 13

## *Expecting Applause!*

✦

### *How to Deal with People Who Don't Want You to Change*

Transforming yourself takes work. When you push yourself to do it, you would like people around you to appreciate and support your efforts. Many times they do, but not always. Some people have a stake in keeping you just as you are.

Marlene found that out when she took a major leap forward in her quest to meet men and eventually find a husband. As shy as Marlene is, it terrified her to hit the Submit button on the Match.com Web site. But she did hit, posting her biography and two photos of herself on the popular Internet dating service. To her amazement, three men responded the very first day.

The biggest surprise was her roommate's reaction. Joannie, also in her late twenties and shy, talks incessantly about meeting men. She regales Marlene with detailed fantasies of the big weddings they will have, the kids they will raise, and stuff like that. When Marlene told Joannie that she's taken the bull by the horns and signed up with Match.com, Joannie did nothing but trash the whole idea, even though Joannie herself once said that was something the two of them really should do.

"Forget it. Guys who use dating services are losers," Joannie argued.

Marlene shrugged and said she didn't think so. She even reminded Joannie that Amy, Joannie's favorite cousin, had just married a guy both of them thought was neat. She also reminded Joannie that Amy and her new husband had met online. Joannie escalated her assault.

"I'm telling you. There's a lot of crazies out there, Marlene. For all you know, you're sitting in Starbucks across from Jack the Ripper. Next time, you meet for a movie. Afterwards, he walks you to your car. Zap! Right there in the parking structure, he slits your throat!"

Joannie's near hysteria puzzled Marlene. She was also more than a little hurt that her best friend was not congratulating her for finally doing something besides just sitting around and talking about meeting men.

Let's push the Pause button on this little scenario. Why is Joannie trying to stop her best friend from making a move that might help her friend fulfill her deeply held desire to find a husband? What's really going on here? Marlene was wondering that, too.

The answer is that she is afraid Marlene might meet somebody. (Of course, Joannie would never admit this to Marlene and maybe not even to herself). Joannie sees it clearly. Marlene falls in love, runs off with some man, and builds an exciting new life while she is left behind, alone and miserable. Being too scared to make any serious effort on her own to find a man, Joannie tries any tactic that might put the skids on Marlene moving forward.

Joannie is not an awful person. In fact, she loves Marlene. However, her racing mind, haunted by images of their cozy life together going up in smoke, is fighting Marlene to protect her own life. I must tell you, if we could inject Joannie with a bit of truth serum, she must confess that, deep in her heart, she knows Marlene has made a good move.

If you start making serious changes, like Marlene, you may find yourself dealing with someone, possibly even more than one person, who is saying and doing things designed to discourage you. What makes people do that? Especially a person who claims to care about you? When changing your ways threatens another person with some type of loss, that is when you will get resistance. One of Joannie's big threats was the loss of Marlene as a roommate and companion. If Marlene moved out, she would be left behind, lonely with no one to talk to or go places with. Marlene's move also threatened Joannie with a loss of self-esteem for doing nothing to meet men. As long as both she and Marlene did nothing together, everything was okay. Now, despite Marlene's shyness and fears, she had screwed up the courage to take action. That left Joannie, the paralyzed member of their duo, feeling both alone and exposed as pathetically weak. However, if she could get Marlene off Match.com, the problem would bury itself. Things would then return to normal.

Let's take a closer look at this notion of threat of loss because obviously not all threats and losses are created equal. Suppose you are someone who caters to everyone else's needs and tends to ignore your own. You volunteer to run errands, go where others want to go, and do what they want to do. You have come to a point where you are tired of turning yourself into a pretzel to please other people. You have finally decided it is time to start pleasing yourself. It is a great idea. In fact, it is just what take-charge living is all about—changing in ways that make your life richer and more satisfying.

But what about the people you are inconveniencing by not being at their beck and call anymore? Understandably, they miss the things you used to do for them. Most will encourage what is best for you anyway. However, you may find some who resent the inconvenience you've caused. Beyond inconvenience, you changing may actually threaten people with a loss, perhaps loss of control, loss of seeing themselves as more important, or even loss because they felt entitled to your servitude. Consciously or not, these people are reacting as if "How dare reliable Harriet or Harry decide to play by a new set of rules!" You'll hear about it, too. "You used to be so thoughtful Harriet/Harry. What's come over you?" That's at the light end. A heavy-duty attack might be, "I can't believe what a selfish bitch/bastard you turned into, Harriet/Harry. Try thinking of someone besides yourself for a change." I will later discuss how to handle such pressure without sacrificing your own goals for change.

Feeling inconvenienced is a relatively minor loss. However, people sometimes feel threatened by a deeper loss. Say your spouse is a control freak, a person who has dictated how every little thing is done around the house for years. You've decided you've had enough and start doing things more your own way. That threatens your spouse's self-image, a belief in his or her importance as the person with ultimate authority in your family, the one whose wishes must be obeyed. Believe me, people do not let go of such self-serving ideas easily. So, anyone in this situation should expect resistance and plan how to face it and deal with it without caving in to the pressure to be your old self.

Fear is sometimes the threat driving someone who is trying to stop you from changing. That is what drove Joannie's resistance. Marlene actively looking for a husband tapped Joannie's fear of abandonment. Marlene joining Match.com also confronted Joannie with fearful thoughts about herself that, namely that Marlene—no not just Marlene—most woman, even shy ones, had more guts than she did when it came to meeting men.

I'm sure you can think of examples, perhaps from your own immediate circle of friends and family, in which one person's changes threaten someone else with loss. That happens when a couple abuses alcohol together, but one decides to quit. It happens when a meek person finally stands up to a bully, or walks out on an abusive relationship, or challenges a boss, or takes action against an intrusive neighbor, or question a doctor's decisions. The list of possible scenarios is endless.

If friends are sometimes not always in our corner when we set out to transform ourselves in some way, imagine people who are not fans of ours in the first place. Those people can really play hardball. I don't say that to scare you, but rather to help. By knowing what to expect, you can prepare for it.

Resistance can appear in many forms. Some are subtle. Others are very direct, even aggressive, or anything in between. For Anne, a college senior working hard to try to lose weight, resistance came from her mother pushing food during her weekend visits home. The mother, a fabulous cook whose own weight is testimony to how much she enjoys her creations, pushes food on anyone who sets foot in her house. Anne's refusals—and it takes willpower to refuse a second helping of her mother's beef bourguignon or pass on luscious banana cream pie—are met with, "Just a taste. Try it. It's delicious. You're thin enough, Annie. The obsession with weight in this country is ridiculous. Here, have a small piece." Her mother then pushes a huge slice Anne's way. Tired of the struggle and determined to stick with her diet, Anne began limiting her visits home. Instead, she spends weekends with friends.

Much meaner was the resistance a woman named Shannon ran into after she checked herself into an inpatient drug treatment program. Having abused both drugs and alcohol for years and recently attempting suicide, eighteen-year-old Shannon was desperate. The program, which incorporated the Alcoholics Anonymous twelve-step approach, was wonderful for her. A fundamental of such programs is the idea that alcoholism is a disease and total abstinence is the only way to deal with it. Typical of such programs, Shannon's requested that families attend certain group therapy sessions. Shannon's parents were divorced, and her mother was out of the country. Her father Amos, a clinical psychologist and flaming alcoholic himself, decided to come. In flagrant disregard of his daughter, the other patients, and the treatment staff, Amos used his considerable verbal skill and clinical knowledge to pontificate about how alcoholism is not a disease and how controlled drinking is completely realistic for them. Why would a father do this to a daughter in such desperate need of help? Amos's resistance and his attempt to smear the program helping Shannon was a self-centered effort to rationalize his own excesses with alcohol. By attacking the program, he could justify his own drinking and not admit to himself that he needed help as much as any patient in the room.

Whatever its form, resistance from others complicates your task. When you're trying to move ahead with changing, you sure don't need discouragement. But if it's there you have to deal with it and move ahead anyway. Here are some things to help you.

## Only One Life to Live

Let's start with the most basic and most obvious point. You only get one life to live. You have a perfect right to take charge of that life. It is you, not others, who need to determine how you want to be and what would make you happiest. Then you pursue being that way. When that means transforming some things about yourself, you do it with or without other people's blessing. Improving yourself by changing your ways does not mean ignoring other people or being insensitive or inconsiderate of them. It also does not mean bowing to their whims and wishes instead of pursing your own goals.

If such thinking represents a radical shift of perspective for you, you may have to work at accepting it. As with all the other changes I've talked about, it is all about planning and practicing. What I said in earlier chapters about cognitive restructuring—changing your thinking to help you change how you act—applies to this issue of your right to pursue your chosen goals despite resistance from people who feel threatened by you changing. You may want to review Chapter 8 where all of that is discussed and apply it to the notion of your right to chart the course of your life.

Your job, when you sense resistance from others, is to stay on your chosen course of change. Try to deal as directly and constructively as you can with anyone trying to stop you. Whatever you do, do not let them stop you.

A woman named Jenny had to be proactive, that is, she had to initiate a confrontation with two people who were making her miserable by protecting the current state of affairs. The source of Jenny's unhappiness was allowing her difficult mother-in-law, Sara, to push her and her children around. Sara insisted on having Sunday dinner with her son, Ron, Jenny, and their two children at Jenny and Ron's house. Inevitably, she turned these occasions into a critique of Jenny and how she raised her children. In a typical afternoon, Sara might point a finger at Jenny for sloppy housekeeping, spending too much time at work, the chicken being dry, little Bobby's table manners, Suzie's messy hair, and the children's school being inadequate. Even Sparky the dog's unkempt fur offended her.

When Jenny cried and complained, as she invariably did after Sara went home, Ron sang his usual song. There was nothing they could do about it. His poor mother was a widow. They needed to be kind and nice.

"Just go along with it, Jen. She means well. It's just my mother's way."

Ron knew Jenny was right to complain, but his mother had always intimidated him. That was the real reason he was set against Jenny saying anything.

Ron's resistance was self-serving. The idea of Jenny changing threatened him with loss of the status quo, which meant the possibility of his mother blowing up.

Only Jenny had reached her limit. She first dealt with Ron, explaining calmly, but firmly, that she was done subjecting herself to Sara's put-downs and intended to tell Sara so. Predictably, Ron tried arguing with her, but Jenny, although nervous about it, stuck to her plan. In a private meeting, she said clearly to Sara she was unwilling to be spoken to in that manner any longer and there would be no more Sunday dinners in her home if Sara insisted on keeping it up. Sara got the message and curbed her criticism. As often happens when people stand up for themselves, once Jenny set the limits, although Sara still did not like her daughter-in-law very much, she treated Jenny with overall greater respect.

If you have undertaken some personal change and run into resistance from someone else, first assess its significance. How important is this person to you? How big is their issue? Are you merely inconveniencing their life a little, or truly threatening them by doing things differently? If this relationship matters to you, I would urge you to seriously consider talking frankly with the person. Do it in a considerate way, but talk candidly about the resistance you are experiencing. Be sure to specifically request that the person stop it. Depending upon the specifics of your situation and your relationship to this person, you must decide how deep you want to go into your reasons for the change you are making and your feelings about their reactions. In any case, it's critical that you make it clear that you intend to go forward with the changes. Then stick to your guns and maintain your position.

I'm not saying that's easy. People trying to prevent you from changing are people who feel threatened that your growth means their loss. Not surprisingly, some can be quite difficult to deal with. However, this is your life we're talking about. Your one and only life. Unless you are willing to remain stuck and condemned to a way of a life you do not like, it is imperative you stick to your plan once you have decided it is best for you to change.

Resistance from another person implies conflict because you are not doing what they want. Joannie got testy with Marlene about Internet dating. Ron fought with Jenny to take abuse from his mother instead of confronting her. Conflict—especially when the other person is important to you—may cause you to feel anxiety, guilt, anger, or frustration. That is uncomfortable. Remember, despite uncomfortable negative reactions, you can still move ahead with change. You do not have to listen to negative feelings if doing so keeps you repeating patterns of behavior that do not pay off.

I am not minimizing the compelling nature of negative feelings. As I have often said, when your feelings are not constructive, you must force yourself to act contrary to what they are telling you to do. That may not be easy, but it can be done. The more you practice not taking bad advice from negative feelings, the easier it gets. My bottom line message is once you have decided to change, do not cave in to those who may be trying to stop you. Trust your decision, and continue forging ahead. You have a perfect right to forge ahead you know, to transform yourself into the person you want to be.

Forging ahead is easier if you have people supporting what you are trying to do. In the face of someone who wants to stop you from changing, encouragement and support from friends is invaluable for staying with your program and moving ahead. I strongly urge you to contact the people you know are in your corner. Line up friends who will be there when you need a pep talk. Tell them what's up, the changes you're trying to make. Don't be shy. Openly ask for their support.

If you normally wait for others to reach out, please don't this time. Take the lead. Pick up the phone, send e-mail, or visit. Being able to call people you know who support the changes you are trying to make can make a huge difference, sometimes the difference between success and failure. As The Beatles famously sang many years ago, "I get by with a little help from my friends." Please take that to heart. Get a little or a lot of help from your friends. Keep sharp as to who your real friends are. As a dear friend wisely counseled many years ago, "Don't look for comfort from the source of your oppression."

I have been talking about the value of social support for dealing with people who do not want you to change. However, the benefits of positive relationships go far beyond that. Scientists have shown that social support can even have a positive impact on your immune system. Talk about a mind-body connection! Not only does social support promote health, it sometimes actually prolongs life. Don't play Lone Ranger. Support from your friends is free. It feels good, and it is accessible. Let them help you work your way toward change.

# 14

## *One Hit Leads to Another*

### *How to Make Yours a Lifetime of Empowerment*

Just like *My Fair Lady's* Eliza Doolittle, you play the starring role in your own life's show. Recasting that role is what this book has been all about. Recasting starts with making one specific change.

Let's say your target for change is recasting your role at work because you know your career is stuck unless you can begin speaking up and promoting ideas. Let's also say you take up that challenge. By carefully following all six acts of the take-charge living program, you become much more dynamic and impressive at work. That would be success enough, wouldn't it? While you were changing at work, something else in you was changing as well—arguably something bigger, better, and even more important.

You may remember that I said the only thing that convinces our brains to let go of the false belief that it is too dangerous, difficult, or beyond our ability to change is to see us actually do it. People resist the idea that, for change to happen, they must act first without feeling ready because that feels counterintuitive. Nonetheless, that's how it is.

In my imagined scenario, not only have you become more dynamic at work, your brain has been observing you make this change, understanding full well that you've broken a long-standing pattern of keeping good ideas to yourself out of fear you might sound stupid if you speak up. In view of your new success, your brain is sizing you up in a somewhat different light, as if it is telling itself, "Well, what do you know, she can speak up and push her ideas after all! Nothing bad is happening from doing that. In fact, all this feels very good."

What's more, your brain puts this new information to good use. The next time you want to recast something about how you run your life, your brain, which is trying to protect you, instead of warning you against the idea, is more likely to entertain the possibility that, because you changed successfully once before, you might very well do it again. And so it goes. With each success at changing something you do not like about yourself or handling a situation in a new, better way, you build confidence because your brain increasingly encourages instead of discourages you.

This change is about much more than becoming more assertive at work. Now we are talking about you gradually developing an entire new philosophy, a whole new outlook about how you can and intend to run your life. What I'm saying is that by continually practicing the take-charge living approach, it eventually becomes your everyday way of living. You come to a new understanding and belief that, regardless of which situations you confront (good ones or troubled ones), you can choose how it is best for you to respond instead of repeating old patterns of reacting, which were not getting you where you wanted to go.

This learning process develops over time as you practice using the take-charge living approach to handle a variety of different issues more effectively than you did in the past. As with learning anything, the more you practice, the quicker you get good at it and enjoy its rewards. The key is taking action.

Action can mean many different things—being more assertive, ending bad relationships, pursuing career goals, taming a temper, improving how you talk to people, eating healthy, becoming less self-critical, setting limits, exercising, being honest—or any one of a hundred other changes that would improve your life. Whatever your specific needs for change, lots of research shows that people who take action in the face of some obstacle or difficulty are both psychologically and physically healthier. They sometimes even live longer than people who are stuck in a rut that they passively accept as their lot in life. Letting circumstance, fate, or other people determine things for you is not a healthy way to live.

Start small if you need to, but start! You must begin to take action if you want things to change. Don't wait to feel like taking your first steps before you get going. As I keep saying, it does not work that way. Action comes first. Feelings change afterwards. As I also keep reminding you, the action we are talking about is you working at some personal change in how you think, feel, and act. Take-charge living is never about trying to maneuver others into changing while you hang on to your old ways.

I will wrap up this chapter with three helpful suggestions to keep in mind as you work the take-charge living program. The first is to not expect a perfect performance from yourself, either when you practice the new behavior at home or try it in the world. Changing something personal is a learning process. Like other learning, it happens in steps. Instead of getting discouraged, expect your new performance will be initially awkward, stiff, or off-target. That is exactly the reason take-charge living builds in practice sessions. You must keep learning and fine-tuning.

The second suggestion is keeping your sense of humor as you try new ways of thinking and acting. Change is work. However, getting overly intense or, worse, self-critical only makes it harder to continue. Be a friend to yourself. Giggle at some of your awkward attempts. Nothing says you must be deadly to change. The third suggestion is giving yourself lots of pats on the back for effort. Appreciate that it is gutsy both for you to admit you need to change, and to act on that knowledge. You deserve to pat yourself on the back, not just once, but every step of the way. Please remind yourself to do that.

# *Conclusion: Taking a Bow*

✦

## *How to Appreciate What You've Accomplished*

We're nearing the end of our journey together, and I say this with a certain amount of sadness. In writing these pages, you have come to feel very real to me. I care deeply what happens to you because of reading this book. I wish I could ask if I have sold you on making take-charge living your way of life. Of course, I understand different readers will have different degrees of commitment to working at change. However, every one of you deserves to take a bow for seriously considering doing so by reading this book. That is a start.

My guess is that most of you buy the basic idea of take-charge living. The issue for some may be believing you can do it. I believe you can. I will tell you why I think you should believe that as well.

By now, we have hopefully dispensed with a couple basic, critical issues. The first: Are our personalities so locked in by the time we reach adult life that real change in the way we think, feel, and respond is impossible? As I explained at the outset, change is not only possible, but we are hardwired to be in an ongoing change process. Survival requires adjustment and change in response to the information we steadily receive and process both from inside ourselves as well as from the world around us. The challenge is guiding that change, as opposed to passively letting internal and external forces reshape us. The seventeenth-century Dutch philosopher Baruch Spinoza felt so strongly about the issue that he declared people who do not learn to take control of their thoughts and feelings are in a state of human bondage.

Even allowing that people can and even must change, do they really have meaningful choices to make about those changes? Can they really choose how they will think, feel, and behave? Foreign as that idea may be to some readers, my answer is an unequivocal yes. As long as more than one possible way exists to respond to a given situation, you have a choice. Please ponder that sentence. Let it sink in. Isn't that what this whole book has been about, that is, you really do have a choice?

But—and this is a big "but"—you only have a choice if you believe you do. Believing in choices is what leads to action. Not believing you have choices leaves you stuck in the grips of attitudes, ideas, feelings, and behaviors that promote inaction. Then nothing changes, and you settle for a lesser life.

So now, I bid you good-bye. My final reminder is that take-charge living is a gift only you can give yourself. It certainly helps to have supportive people around you, but the choice to be the skipper of your own life is ultimately yours alone to make. I have faith you can do it. I would love to hear how things turn out.[1]

---

1 You can send word at www.take-chargeliving.com.

www.ingramcontent.com/pod-product-compliance
Ingram Content Group UK Ltd.
Pitfield, Milton Keynes, MK11 3LW, UK
UKHW041945190726
13854UKWH00004B/1798